ing Barnet

**Everyman's Poetry**

*Everyman, I will go with thee,
and be thy guide*

# George Herbert

Selected and edited by D. J. ENRIGHT

EVERYMAN

J. M. Dent · London

This edition first published by Everyman Paperbacks in 1996
Selection, introduction and other critical apparatus
© J. M. Dent 1996

J. M. Dent
Orion Publishing Group
Orion House
5 Upper St Martin's Lane
London WC2H 9EA

Typeset by Deltatype Ltd, Ellesmere Port, Cheshire
Printed in Great Britain by
The Guernsey Press Co. Ltd, Guernsey, C.I.

British Library Cataloguing-in-Publication
Data is available upon request.

ISBN 0 460 87795 X

# Contents

# Note on the Author and Editor

GEORGE HERBERT, the fifth son of Richard and Magdalen Herbert, was born on 3 April 1593 in Montgomery in Wales into an aristocratic family. The head of the family, after the death of his father in 1596, was his brother Edward, later Lord Herbert of Cherbury, also a notable poet and a philosopher. George Herbert was educated at Westminster School and Trinity College, Cambridge. His first poems to be published, in 1612, were two memorial poems in Latin on the death of Prince Henry, the eldest son of James I. In 1616 Herbert was elected a major fellow of Trinity, in 1618 he was appointed Reader in Rhetoric at Cambridge, and in 1620 he was elected Public Orator. In 1624 and 1625 he represented Montgomery in Parliament. In 1626 he was appointed prebendary of Leighton Bromswold in Huntingdonshire, near Little Gidding, and in April 1630 became Rector of Bemerton, near Salisbury; he was ordained priest the following September. The previous year, 1629, he had married Jane Danvers, his stepfather's cousin. Herbert died of consumption on 1 March 1633, shortly before his fortieth birthday. *The Temple*, which contains nearly all his surviving English poems, was published posthumously the same year.

D. J. ENRIGHT has taught in universities overseas and worked in publishing in London. Among his publications are several novels and books of criticism and memoirs. His *Collected Poems* appeared in paperback in 1987 (Oxford University Press). He has edited *A Choice of Milton's Verse* (Faber, 1975), Johnson's *History of Rasselas* (Penguin, 1976) and George Eliot's *Impressions of Theophrastus Such* (Everyman Paperbacks, 1995), and compiled a number of anthologies, including *The Oxford Book of Death* (Oxford University Press, 1983), *The Oxford Book of Friendship* (with David Rawlinson [Oxford University Press, 1991]) and *The Oxford Book of the Supernatural* (Oxford University Press, 1994).

# Chronology of Herbert's Life

| Year | Life |
|------|------|
| 1593 | Born (3 April) in Montgomery in Wales, the fifth son of Richard and Magdalen Herbert |
| 1596 | Death of father, survived by his wife, seven sons and three daughters. The eldest son, Edward, matriculates at University College, Oxford |
| 1599 | Edward Herbert marries a cousin, Mary Herbert |
| 1605 | Attends Westminster School |

# Chronology of his Times

| Year | Artistic Context | Historical Events |
| --- | --- | --- |
| 1593 | Birth of Walton<br>Death of Marlowe | |
| 1595 | Sidney, *Apologie for Poetrie*<br>Spenser, *Amoretti, Epithalamion*<br>Shakespeare's *A Midsummer Night's Dream* first (?) acted<br>Shakespeare's *Richard II* first acted<br>Swan Theatre built | |
| 1596 | Spenser, *Faerie Queene*, Books IV–VI, *Four Hymns*<br>*The Merchant of Venice* first (?) acted | |
| 1597 | Bacon, first ten *Essays* | |
| 1599 | Death of Spenser<br>Shakespeare's *Julius Caesar, Henry V* first acted<br>Globe Theatre opened | Birth of Cromwell |
| 1600 | Shakespeare's *Hamlet* first (?) acted | |
| 1601 | Marriage of Donne to Anne More<br>Shakespeare's *Twelfth Night* first acted | Execution of Essex; Lancelot Andrewes appointed Dean of Westminster |
| 1603 | | Death of Elizabeth I; accession of James I |
| 1604 | Shakespeare's *Othello* first acted | |
| 1605 | Bacon, *Advancement of Learning* | Gunpowder Plot; birth of Sir Thomas Browne |

| *Year* | *Life* |
|--------|--------|
| 1608 | Mother marries Sir John Danvers |
| 1609 | Matriculates at Trinity College, Cambridge |
| 1612 | On the death of the heir apparent, Prince Henry, Herbert contributes two memorial poems in Latin, his first verses to be published; takes his BA degree |
| 1614 | Elected minor fellow of Trinity College; pursues studies in classics and divinity |
| 1616 | Elected major fellow of Trinity College |
| 1618 | Appointed Reader in Rhetoric at Cambridge. Edward Herbert appointed ambassador in Paris |
| 1620 | Elected Public Orator at Cambridge (to 1628) |

| Year | Artistic Context | Historical Events |
|---|---|---|
| 1606 | Shakespeare's *Macbeth, King Lear* first acted<br>Jonson's *Volpone* first acted<br>Tourneur's *The Revenger's Tragedy* first (?) acted | |
| 1608 | Birth of Milton | |
| 1609 | Shakespeare, *Sonnets* | |
| 1610 | Jonson's *The Alchemist* first acted | Galileo improves the refracting telescope and reports his observations |
| 1611 | The King James (Authorized) Version of the Bible<br>Shakespeare's *The Winter's Tale, The Tempest* first acted<br>Chapman's translation of *The Iliad* completed | |
| 1613 | Birth of Crashaw | |
| 1614 | Ralegh, *The History of the World*<br>Webster, *The Duchess of Malfi* first (?) acted | |
| 1615 | Donne ordained | |
| 1616 | Death of Shakespeare<br>Jonson, *Works* | |
| 1618 | Birth of Cowley | Execution of Ralegh; Bacon appointed Lord Chancellor |
| 1619 | | Lancelot Andrewes appointed Bishop of Winchester |
| 1620 | Bacon, *Novum Organum* | |
| 1621 | Burton, *The Anatomy of Melancholy*<br>Births of Marvell, Vaughan | Bacon impeached. Donne appointed Dean of St Paul's |

| Year | Life |
|------|------|
| 1624 | Elected to represent Montgomery in Parliament (also in 1625). Edward Herbert publishes *De Veritate* in Paris |
| 1626 | Appointed prebendary in Huntingdonshire, near Little Gidding. He contributes a memorial poem in Latin on the death of Bacon |
| 1627 | Death of mother; the funeral sermon, delivered by Donne, was accompanied when published by commemorative poems including Herbert's *Memoriae Matris Sacrum* |
| 1629 | Marriage to his stepfather's cousin, Jane Danvers. Edward Herbert raised to the peerage as Lord Herbert of Cherbury |
| 1630 | Becomes Rector at Bemerton, near Salisbury, in April; ordained priest in September |
| 1633 | Dies of consumption, on 1 March, shortly before his fortieth birthday |
| 1633 | *The Temple*, published posthumously |
| 1640 | *Outlandish Proverbs* (enlarged edition, as *Jacula Prudentum*, 1651) |
| 1652 | *A Priest to the Temple*, part of *Herbert's Remains* |

| Year | Artistic Context | Historical Events |
|------|-----------------|-------------------|
| 1623 | The First Folio Shakespeare | |
| 1625 | Bacon dedicates his *Translation of Certaine Psalmes* to Herbert Death of Webster | Death of James I; accession of Charles I; Nicholas Ferrar settles at Little Gidding, in Huntingdonshire |
| 1626 | Deaths of Bacon and Andrewes Birth of Aubrey | |
| 1628 | Harvey's treatise on the circulation of the blood Birth of Bunyan | |
| 1629 | Andrewes, *XCVI Sermons* (posthumously) | |
| 1630 | | Birth of Prince Charles (later King Charles II) |
| 1631 | Death of Donne Birth of Dryden | |
| 1633 | Donne, *Poems* (posthumously) | William Laud appointed Archbishop of Canterbury |

# Introduction

George Herbert is undeniably a devotional poet, devoted to Christ and to the Church as Christ's representative on earth, yet his poetry has an energy, inventiveness and intellectual depth and edge usually missing from what we think of as devotional verse. At their best, which is most of the time, the poems that make up *The Temple* are flawless and irresistible, and – for the tone of voice is immediately recognizable as his and his alone – unique. They are among the very finest we have in English; in them we hear a man pleading with God or arguing with him, or disputing with himself, but always talking to other men.

Herbert came of an aristocratic family, conversant with the arts of government, the Court and the mind, and in 1620 he was elected Public Orator at Cambridge, 'the finest place in the University', he said, and an acknowledged stepping-stone to high state office. A number of his patrons, including James I, died in subsequent years, and – although for a man of his obvious qualities all hopes of preferment would hardly have vanished for that reason – he was ordained a deacon in 1626. 'My birth and spirit rather took/The way that takes the town', he writes in a poem in which the dichotomy of town and gown is wholly apposite. But it would be wrong to make much of the conflict between Herbert's worldly ambitions and his impulse towards a life of religion. We see nothing in him akin to the sharp division in the elder poet between Jack Donne the gallant and John Donne the Dean of St Paul's, 'Apollo's first, at last, the true God's priest', as a contemporary described him. In a letter to his mother written in his sixteenth year Herbert declared that his 'poor abilities in poetry shall be all and ever consecrated to God's glory'; and in 'Submission' he notes, wryly but not resentfully, that 'Perhaps great places and thy praise/Do not so well agree.' For him, the real conflict lay elsewhere, in the crucial relation between the glory of God and his 'poor abilities', in the shame of falling short in his profession, but not of yearning after a more exalted one.

Herbert's main themes, touched on in a multiplicity of connec-
tions, are the Incarnation, the Passion and the Redemption.
Against the debt owed to Christ stand both the unseemliness of
man's disobedience and the gross inadequacy of his obedience.
While Herbert could have had little to reproach himself with on the
first score, tender of conscience though he was, the burden of
indebtedness lay heavy on him. 'Then for thy passion – I will do for
that –/Alas, my God, I know not what.' Hence flow the tears, the
sighs and groans, recurrent in his verse. Modern readers may find it
hard to comprehend this deep sense of insufficiency and failure,
especially in one who in a short life achieved much as a priest (his
brief ministry became a classic example for the English Church) and
much more as a poet. Yet similar feelings are surely a part of our
own lives and experience, evoked by different factors it may be, and
intensified by the natural pride we share with him. The self-
examination and self-discovery so exquisitely and unaffectedly
pursued through *The Temple* are not restricted to followers of a
religious faith. Herbert's struggles and his dejection of spirit are
ours, despite ours arising in circumstances of another nature. We
too wish to be of use, however modestly, as a tree harbours birds or
bees make honey. We are fortunate if we find something compara-
ble to the resolution he arrived at, his eventual acquiescence in his
place and status in creation.

Herbert was in some degree a 'metaphysical poet', of the school of
Donne, in that his imagery and allusions, largely drawn from
church furniture, flowers, perfumes, farming, stars, the law,
commerce, medicine, architecture and (above all) music, are often
surprising, 'unexpected'. Not, however, startling by virtue of their
ingenuity, learnedness or outlandishness, but rather because of
their apparently incongruous homeliness. Nonetheless there is
what critics have called a 'dormant complexity' there, a 'boring
down' into a traditional topic or instance to discover 'new veins of
meaning'. Herbert was never content with surfaces or platitudes.
The seeming ease, the lyrical flow, can blind us to the presence of
what T. S. Eliot termed 'brain-work', adding to the 'heart-work' and
'heaven-work' ascribed to Herbert by Richard Baxter in the late
seventeenth century.

Of Herbert's use of the homely, Helen C. White has observed that
he 'employs it to domesticate wonder, to bring the remote home to
hearth and bosom, to give to the general, the sharp incidence of the

particular, the breath-taking freshness of the just-happened'. Indeed, that effect of the 'just-happened', the freshness, the bringing home to us of what we may have thought we knew already, so that abstract acquaintance turns into immediate experience, is the very heart of Herbert's genius. In its eighteen lines, that perfect parable-poem 'Love (III)', the closing poem in *The Temple* and in this selection from it, surpasses whole volumes of theological commentary: it does not merely inform, expound or elaborate, it draws us into the event. If Christ had left us poems, we think, this would have been among the most potent.

A passage from Izaak Walton's *Life*, concerning Herbert's appointment to the rectorship of Bemerton, near Salisbury, in 1630, is to the point. Herbert delivered his first sermon 'after a most florid manner, both with great learning and eloquence. But, at the close, told them, "That should not be his constant way of preaching; for since Almighty God does not intend to lead men to heaven by hard questions, he would not therefore fill their heads with unnecessary notions; but that for their sakes, his language and his expressions should be more plain and practical in his future sermons." ' The hard questions are there in his poems, and hard answers too, but limpidly and dramatically set out: 'A verse may find him, who a sermon flies,/And turn delight into a sacrifice.' *A Priest to the Temple*, Herbert's vade-mecum for the country parson, is eminently practical: in it he advises that a sermon shouldn't last more than an hour, since if the listener hasn't profited by then he will profit even less thereafter, and from not relishing what is being said he will turn to loathing it. He also observes that the parson will sometimes tell his congregation stories, as the text he is preaching on suggests, 'for them also men heed, and remember better than exhortations'. The same spirit pervades such poems, or stories, or plays in miniature, as 'Redemption', 'The Quip', 'Peace', and (anticipating Bunyan, and combining the popular with the courtly) 'The Pilgrimage'. There, as in 'Love (III)', where the poet, 'unkind, ungrateful', confesses, 'Ah my dear,/I cannot look on thee', and Love replies with a smile, 'Who made the eyes but I?', lie hard questions, partly buried, and hard answers, the latter softened on occasion by tenderness.

One form of compressed 'story' common in the poems is the proverbial or aphoristic saying: 'He pares his apple, that will cleanly feed', 'Wouldst thou both eat thy cake, and have it?', 'Fractures well cur'd make us more strong'. And Herbert delights us with invigorating touches of humour: in 'Whitsunday', the gifts bestowed by the Holy Spirit have virtually transformed the earth into heaven and the stars come down to see if they can better their wages by finding jobs there. If that is thought to smack of whimsy, more sturdy is 'Vanity', in which the astronomer inspects the spheres from all angles as if he were planning to buy one of them; while the chemist, admitted to their bedchamber, strips the principles of matter naked and gives them a piece of his mind. A few phrases fix a brilliant picture of scientists at work, both amusing and, with a light touch, admonishing their busy self-importance. More daringly still, in 'Doomsday', the awakened dust rubs its eyes and the limbs nudge one another, asking, 'Live you, brother?'

Here and there the scales are weighed clumsily, too deliberately, against earthly pleasures, however innocuous, as obstacles to heavenly bliss and the struggle to fit oneself for it. 'Then silly soul take heed; for earthly joy/Is but a bubble, and makes thee a boy' is slackly phrased, a mechanical rebuke, and likewise (in another poem not included here) 'What is this weary world, this meat and drink,/That chains us by the teeth so fast?' These are rare lapses in tension, amply offset by the linguistic and moral muscularity of 'The Quiddity', the poetic manifesto, staunch yet urbane, of 'Jordan (I)' ('I envy no man's nightingale or spring'), the embattled aplomb of 'The Quip' and 'The Storm' ('Poets have wrong'd poor storms: such days are best'), the sudden earthy shock of 'My friend may spit upon my curious floor' or 'Death, puffing at the door,/Blows all the dust about the floor', the desolation of 'O that thou shouldst give dust a tongue/To cry to thee,/And then not hear it crying!', the brave rallying in 'It cannot be/That I am he/On whom thy tempests fell all night', the forcefully justified revolt of the heart in 'The Collar' and its final and just capitulation, the sheer happiness of 'Easter', and the joyous assurance of 'Love is that liquor sweet and most divine,/Which my God feels as blood; but I, as wine.'

These and other poems, which waken a special, intimate pleasure in us and compel a perhaps not altogether ready assent (or perhaps a rueful sense of loss), bear out Seamus Heaney's comment that, while Herbert surrendered himself to a framework of belief and an institutional religion, his personality was such 'that he could dwell in amity with doctrine, writing a poetry which was intellectually pure, emotionally robust and entirely authentic'. The

human psyche has not changed radically since Herbert's day. He is
a poet, if not for all seasons, then for seasons which most of us live
through at one time or another, and perhaps repeatedly.

                                                    D. J. ENRIGHT

# Note on the Text

The text of the poems is based on F. E. Hutchinson's *The Works of George Herbert* (Oxford: Clarendon Press, 1941). Spelling has been modernized except where Herbert's words have a special significance ('chymick': alchemist as well as chemist) and when rhyme requires the original form ('strow'd': strewed), and also in such 'visual rhymes' as 'best'/'opprest'.

Words such as 'loved', 'looked', 'scourged', 'lodged', spelt thus, are pronounced as two syllables, and 'reversed', 'dispersed' etc. as three. When the *e* is elided, the word is pronounced as one syllable, e.g. 'heav'n', 'ev'n', and likewise 'lov'd', 'vi'd' (vied), 'ti'd' (tied), 'cri'd' (cried), 'di'd' (died), or as two or three syllables: 'rev'rend', 'carri'd', 'untun'd', 'multipli'd', 'consider'd'. Similarly 'th' one' is monosyllabic, 'th' other' disyllabic, etc.

# George Herbert

# The Thanksgiving

Oh King of grief! (a title strange, yet true,
    To thee of all kings only due),
Oh King of wounds! how shall I grieve for thee,
    Who in all grief preventest me?
Shall I weep blood? why, thou hast wept such store
    That all thy body was one door.
Shall I be scourged, flouted, boxed, sold?
    'Tis but to tell the tale is told.
*My God, my God, why dost thou part from me?*
    Was such a grief as cannot be.
Shall I then sing, skipping thy doleful story,
    And side with thy triumphant glory?
Shall thy strokes be my stroking? thorns, my flower?
    Thy rod, my posy? cross, my bower?
But how then shall I imitate thee, and
    Copy thy fair, though bloody hand?
Surely I will revenge me on thy love,
    And try who shall victorious prove.
If you dost give me wealth, I will restore
    All back unto thee by the poor.
If thou dost give me honour, men shall see,
    The honour doth belong to thee.
I will not marry; or, if she be mine,
    She and her children shall be thine.
My bosom friend, if he blaspheme thy name,
    I will tear thence his love and fame.
One half of me being gone, the rest I give
    Unto some chapel, die or live.
As for thy passion – But of that anon,
    When with the other I have done.
For thy predestination I'll contrive,
    That three years hence, if I survive,
I'll build a spital, or mend common ways,
    But mend mine own without delays.
Then I will use the works of thy creation,

As if I us'd them but for fashion.
The world and I will quarrel; and the year
    Shall not perceive, that I am here.
My music shall find thee, and ev'ry string
    Shall have his attribute to sing;
That all together may accord in thee,
    And prove one God, one harmony.
If thou shalt give me wit, it shall appear,
    If thou hast giv'n it me, 'tis here.
Nay, I will read thy book, and never move
    Till I have found therein thy love,
Thy art of love, which I'll turn back on thee:
    O my dear Saviour, victory!
Then for thy passion – I will do for that –
    Alas, my God, I know not what.

## The Reprisal

I have consider'd it, and find
There is no dealing with thy mighty passion:
For though I die for thee, I am behind;
    My sins deserve the condemnation.

O make me innocent, that I
May give a disentangled state and free:
And yet thy wounds still my attempts defy,
    For by thy death I die for thee.

Ah! was it not enough that thou
By thy eternal glory didst outgo me?
Couldst thou not grief's sad conquests me allow,
    But in all vict'ries overthrow me?

Yet by confession will I come
Into thy conquest: though I can do nought
Against thee, in thee I will overcome
    The man, who once against thee fought.

# The Agony

Philosophers have measur'd mountains,
Fathom'd the depths of seas, of states, and kings,
Walk'd with a staff to heav'n, and traced fountains:
    But there are two vast, spacious things,
The which to measure it doth more behove:
Yet few there are that sound them, Sin and Love.

Who would know Sin, let him repair
Unto Mount Olivet; there shall he see
A man so wrung with pains, that all his hair,
    His skin, his garments bloody be.
Sin is that press and vice, which forceth pain
To hunt his cruel food through ev'ry vein.

Who knows not Love, let him assay
And taste that juice, which on the cross a pike
Did set again abroach; then let him say
    If ever he did taste the like.
Love is that liquor sweet and most divine,
Which my God feels as blood; but I, as wine.

# Redemption

Having been tenant long to a rich Lord,
    Not thriving, I resolved to be bold,
    And make a suit unto him, to afford
A new small-rented lease, and cancel th' old.
In heaven at his manor I him sought:
    They told me there, that he was lately gone
    About some land, which he had dearly bought
Long since on earth, to take possession.
I straight return'd, and knowing his great birth,

Sought him accordingly in great resorts;
  In cities, theatres, gardens, parks, and courts:
At length I heard a ragged noise and mirth
  Of thieves and murderers: there I him espi'd,
  Who straight, *Your suit is granted*, said, and di'd.

# Easter

Rise heart; thy Lord is risen. Sing his praise
                    Without delays,
Who takes thee by the hand, that thou likewise
                    With him mayst rise:
That, as his death calcined thee to dust,
His life may make thee gold, and much more, just.

Awake, my lute, and struggle for thy part
                    With all thy art.
The cross taught all wood to resound his name,
                    Who bore the same.
His stretched sinews taught all strings, what key
Is best to celebrate this most high day.

Consort both heart and lute, and twist a song
                    Pleasant and long:
Or, since all music is but three parts vi'd
                    And multipli'd,
O let thy blessed Spirit bear a part,
And make up our defects with his sweet art.

  I got me flowers to strew thy way,
  I got me boughs off many a tree:
  But thou wast up by break of day,
  And brought'st thy sweets along with thee.

The sun arising in the East,
Though he give light, and th' East perfume,
If they should offer to contest
With thy arising, they presume.

Can there be any day but this,
Though many suns to shine endeavour?
We count three hundred, but we miss:
There is but one, and that one ever.

## Easter-wings

Lord, who createdst man in wealth and store,
  Though foolishly he lost the same,
    Decaying more and more,
      Till he became
       Most poor:
       With thee
      O let me rise
    As larks, harmoniously,
  And sing this day thy victories:
Then shall the fall further the flight in me.

My tender age in sorrow did begin:
  And still with sicknesses and shame
    Thou didst so punish sin,
      That I became
       Most thin.
       With thee
      Let me combine
    And feel this day thy victory:
  For, if I imp my wing on thine,
Affliction shall advance the flight in me.

# Sin (I)

Lord, with what care hast thou begirt us round!
Parents first season us: then schoolmasters
   Deliver us to laws; they send us bound
To rules of reason, holy messengers,
Pulpits and Sundays, sorrow dogging sin,
   Afflictions sorted, anguish of all sizes,
   Fine nets and stratagems to catch us in,
Bibles laid open, millions of surprises,
Blessings beforehand, ties of gratefulness,
   The sound of glory ringing in our ears:
   Without, our shame; within, our consciences;
Angels and grace, eternal hopes and fears.
   Yet all these fences and their whole array
   One cunning bosom-sin blows quite away.

# Affliction (I)

When first thou didst entice to thee my heart,
        I thought the service brave:
So many joys I writ down for my part,
        Besides what I might have
Out of my stock of natural delights,
Augmented with thy gracious benefits.

I looked on thy furniture so fine,
        And made it fine to me:
Thy glorious household-stuff did me entwine,
        And tice me unto thee.
Such stars I counted mine: both heav'n and earth
Paid me my wages in a world of mirth.

What pleasures could I want, whose King I served,
        Where joys my fellows were?

Thus argu'd into hopes, my thoughts reserved
        No place for grief or fear.
Therefore my sudden soul caught at the place,
And made her youth and fierceness seek thy face.

At first thou gav'st me milk and sweetnesses;
        I had my wish and way:
My days were strew'd with flowers and happiness;
        There was no month but May.
But with my years sorrow did twist and grow,
And made a party unawares for woe.

My flesh began unto my soul in pain,
        Sicknesses cleave my bones;
Consuming agues dwell in ev'ry vein,
        And tune my breath to groans.
Sorrow was all my soul; I scarce believ'd,
Till grief did tell me roundly, that I liv'd.

When I got health, thou tookst away my life,
        And more; for my friends die:
My mirth and edge was lost; a blunted knife
        Was of more use than I.
Thus thin and lean without a fence or friend,
I was blown through with ev'ry storm and wind.

Whereas my birth and spirit rather took
        The way that takes the town,
Thou didst betray me to a ling'ring book,
        And wrap me in a gown.
I was entangled in the world of strife,
Before I had the power to change my life.

Yet, for I threaten'd oft the siege to raise,
        Not simp'ring all mine age,
Thou often didst with academic praise
        Melt and dissolve my rage.
I took thy sweeten'd pill, till I came where
I could not go away, nor persevere.

Yet lest perchance I should too happy be
          In my unhappiness,
Turning my purge to food, thou throwest me
          Into more sicknesses.
Thus doth thy power cross-bias me, not making
Thine own gift good, yet me from my ways taking.

Now I am here, what thou wilt do with me
          None of my books will show:
I read, and sigh, and wish I were a tree;
          For sure then I should grow
To fruit or shade: at least some bird would trust
Her household to me, and I should be just.

Yet, though thou troublest me, I must be meek;
          In weakness must be stout.
Well, I will change the service, and go seek
          Some other master out.
Ah my dear God! though I am clean forgot,
Let me not love thee, if I love thee not.

# Repentance

Lord, I confess my sin is great;
Great is my sin. Oh! gently treat
With thy quick flower, thy momentary bloom;
          Whose life still pressing
          Is one undressing,
A steady aiming at a tomb.

Man's age is two hours' work, or three:
Each day doth round about us see.
Thus are we to delights: but we are all
          To sorrows old,
          If life be told
From what life feeleth, Adam's fall.

O let thy height of mercy then
Compassionate short-breathed men.
Cut me not off for my most foul transgression:
   I do confess
   My foolishness;
My God, accept of my confession.


Sweeten at length this bitter bowl,
Which thou hast pour'd into my soul;
Thy wormwood turn to health, winds to fair weather:
   For if thou stay,
   I and this day,
As we did rise, we die together.


When thou for sin rebukest man,
Forthwith he waxeth woe and wan:
Bitterness fills our bowels; all our hearts
   Pine, and decay,
   And drop away,
And carry with them th' other parts.


But thou wilt sin and grief destroy;
That so the broken bones may joy,
And tune together in a well-set song,
   Full of his praises,
   Who dead men raises.
Fractures well cur'd make us more strong.


# Prayer (I)


Prayer the Church's banquet, Angels' age,
 God's breath in man returning to his birth,
 The soul in paraphrase, heart in pilgrimage,
The Christian plummet sounding heav'n and earth;
Engine against th' Almighty, sinners' tower,

Reversed thunder, Christ-side-piercing spear,
The six-days' world transposing in an hour,
A kind of tune, which all things hear and fear;
Softness, and peace, and joy, and love, and bliss,
Exalted manna, gladness of the best,
Heaven in ordinary, man well drest,
The milky way, the bird of Paradise,
Church-bells beyond the stars heard, the soul's blood,
The land of spices; something understood.

# Antiphon

CHO: Let all the world in ev'ry corner sing,
*My God and King.*
VERS: The heav'ns are not too high,
His praise may thither fly:
The earth is not too low,
His praises there may grow.

CHO: Let all the world in ev'ry corner sing,
*My God and King.*
VERS: The church with psalms must shout,
No door can keep them out:
But above all, the heart
Must bear the longest part.

CHO: Let all the world in ev'ry corner sing,
*My God and King.*

# Love (I)

Immortal Love, author of this great frame,
  Sprung from that beauty which can never fade:
  How hath man parcell'd out thy glorious name,
And thrown it on that dust which thou hast made,
While mortal love doth all the title gain!
  Which siding with invention, they together
  Bear all the sway, possessing heart and brain
(Thy workmanship), and give thee share in neither.
Wit fancies beauty, beauty raiseth wit:
  The world is theirs; they two play out the game,
  Thou standing by: and though thy glorious name
Wrought our deliverance from th' infernal pit,
  Who sings thy praise? only a scarf or glove
  Doth warm our hands, and make them write of love.

# Love (II)

Immortal Heat, O let thy greater flame
  Attract the lesser to it: let those fires,
  Which shall consume the world, first make it tame;
And kindle in our hearts such true desires,
As may consume our lusts, and make thee way.
  Then shall our hearts pant thee; then shall our brain
  All her invention on thine altar lay,
And there in hymns send back thy fire again.
Our eyes shall see thee, which before saw dust,
  Dust blown by wit, till that they both were blind:
  Thou shalt recover all thy goods in kind,
Who wert disseized by usurping lust:
  All knees shall bow to thee; all wits shall rise,
  And praise him who did make and mend our eyes.

# The Temper

How should I praise thee, Lord! how should my rhymes
　　Gladly engrave thy love in steel,
　　If what my soul doth feel sometimes,
　　　　My soul might ever feel!

Although there were some forty heav'ns, or more,
　　Sometimes I peer above them all;
　　Sometimes I hardly reach a score,
　　　　Sometimes to hell I fall.

O rack me not to such a vast extent;
　　Those distances belong to thee:
　　The world's too little for thy tent,
　　　　A grave too big for me.

Wilt thou meet arms with man, that thou dost stretch
　　A crumb of dust from heav'n to hell?
　　Will great God measure with a wretch?
　　　　Shall he thy stature spell?

O let me, when thy roof my soul hath hid,
　　O let me roost and nestle there:
　　Then of a sinner thou art rid,
　　　　And I of hope and fear.

Yet take thy way; for sure thy way is best:
　　Stretch or contract me, thy poor debter:
　　This is but tuning of my breast,
　　　　To make the music better.

Whether I fly with angels, fall with dust,
　　Thy hands made both, and I am there:
　　Thy power and love, my love and trust
　　　　Make one place ev'rywhere.

# Jordan (I)

Who says that fictions only and false hair
Become a verse? Is there in truth no beauty?
Is all good structure in a winding stair?
May no lines pass, except they do their duty
    Not to a true, but painted chair?

Is it no verse, except enchanted groves
And sudden arbours shadow coarse-spun lines?
Must purling streams refresh a lover's loves?
Must all be veil'd, while he that reads, divines,
    Catching the sense at two removes?

Shepherds are honest people; let them sing:
Riddle who list, for me, and pull for prime:
I envy no man's nightingale or spring;
Nor let them punish me with loss of rhyme,
    Who plainly say, *My God, My King.*

# Employment (I)

    If as a flower doth spread and die,
      Thou wouldst extend me to some good,
  Before I were by frost's extremity
            Nipped in the bud,

    The sweetness and the praise were thine;
      But the extension and the room,
 Which in thy garland I should fill, were mine
            At thy great doom.

    For as thou dost impart thy grace,
    The greater shall our glory be.

The measure of our joys is in this place,
             The stuff with thee.

Let me not languish then, and spend
A life as barren to thy praise
As is the dust, to which that life doth tend,
             But with delays.

All things are busy; only I
Neither bring honey with the bees,
Nor flowers to make that, nor the husbandry
             To water these.

I am no link of thy great chain,
But all my company is a weed.
Lord place me in thy consort; give one strain
             To my poor reed.


# The Holy Scriptures

I

Oh Book! infinite sweetness! Let my heart
   Suck ev'ry letter, and a honey gain,
   Precious for any grief in any part;
To clear the breast, to mollify all pain.
Thou art all health, health thriving till it make
   A full eternity: thou art a mass
   Of strange delights, where we may wish and take.
Ladies, look here; this is the thankful glass,
That mends the looker's eyes: this is the well
   That washes what it shows. Who can endear
   Thy praise too much? thou art heav'n's ledger here,
Working against the states of death and hell.
   Thou art joy's handsel: heav'n lies flat in thee,
   Subject to ev'ry mounter's bended knee.

## II

Oh that I knew how all thy lights combine,
  And the configurations of their glory!
  Seeing not only how each verse doth shine,
But all the constellations of the story.
This verse marks that, and both do make a motion
  Unto a third, that ten leaves off doth lie:
  Then as dispersed herbs do watch a potion,
These three make up some Christian's destiny:
Such are thy secrets, which my life makes good,
  And comments on thee: for in ev'rything
  Thy words do find me out, and parallels bring,
And in another make me understood.
  Stars are poor books, and oftentimes do miss:
  This book of stars lights to eternal bliss.

# Whitsunday

Listen sweet Dove unto my song,
  And spread thy golden wings in me;
  Hatching my tender heart so long,
Till it get wing, and fly away with thee.

Where is that fire which once descended
  On thy apostles? thou didst then
  Keep open house, richly attended,
Feasting all comers by twelve chosen men.

Such glorious gifts thou didst bestow,
  That th' earth did like a heav'n appear;
  The stars were coming down to know
If they might mend their wages, and serve here.

The sun, which once did shine alone,
  Hung down his head, and wish'd for night,

When he beheld twelve suns for one
Going about the world, and giving light.

But since those pipes of gold, which brought
    That cordial water to our ground,
    Were cut and martyr'd by the fault
Of those, who did themselves through their side wound,

Thou shutt'st the door, and keep'st within;
    Scarce a good joy creeps through the chink:
    And if the braves of conqu'ring sin
Did not excite thee, we should wholly sink.

Lord, though we change, thou art the same;
    The same sweet God of love and light:
    Restore this day, for thy great name,
Unto his ancient and miraculous right.

# Grace

My stock lies dead, and no increase
    Doth my dull husbandry improve:
    O let thy graces without cease
            Drop from above!

If still the sun should hide his face,
    Thy house would but a dungeon prove,
    Thy works night's captives: O let grace
            Drop from above!

The dew doth ev'ry morning fall;
    And shall the dew outstrip thy Dove?
    The dew, for which grass cannot call,
            Drop from above.

Death is still working like a mole,
    And digs my grave at each remove:

Let grace work too, and on my soul
   Drop from above.

Sin is still hammering my heart
Unto a hardness, void of love:
Let suppling grace, to cross his art,
   Drop from above.

O come! for thou dost know the way:
Or if to me thou wilt not move,
Remove me, where I need not say,
   *Drop from above.*

# Praise

To write a verse or two is all the praise,
   That I can raise:
    Mend my estate in any ways,
    Thou shalt have more.

I go to church; help me to wings, and I
   Will thither fly;
    Or, if I mount unto the sky,
    I will do more.

Man is all weakness; there is no such thing
   As Prince or King;
    His arm is short: yet with a sling
    He may do more.

An herb distill'd, and drunk, may dwell next door,
   On the same floor,
    To a brave soul: exalt the poor,
    They can do more.

O raise me then! Poor bees, that work all day,
　　　　　Sting my delay,
　　　　Who have a work, as well as they,
　　　　　And much, much more.

# Sin (II)

O that I could a sin once see!
We paint the devil foul, yet he
Hath some good in him, all agree.
Sin is flat opposite to th' Almighty, seeing
It wants the good of *virtue*, and of *being*.

But God more care of us hath had:
If apparitions make us sad,
By sight of sin we should grow mad.
Yet as in sleep we see foul death, and live:
So devils are our sins in perspective.

# Church-music

Sweetest of sweets, I thank you: when displeasure
　　　　　Did through my body wound my mind,
You took me thence, and in your house of pleasure
　　　　　A dainty lodging me assign'd.

Now I in you without a body move,
　　　　　Rising and falling with your wings:
We both together sweetly live and love,
　　　　　Yet say sometimes, *God help poor Kings*.

Comfort, I'll die; for if you post from me,
　　　　　Sure I shall do so, and much more:

But if I travel in your company,
            You know the way to heaven's door.

## Church-lock and Key

I know it is my sin, which locks thine ears,
            And binds thy hands,
Out-crying my requests, drowning my tears;
Or else the chillness of my faint demands.

But as cold hands are angry with the fire,
            And mend it still,
So I do lay the want of my desire,
Not on my sins, or coldness, but thy will.

Yet hear, O God, only for his blood's sake
            Which pleads for me:
For though sins plead too, yet like stones they make
His blood's sweet current much more loud to be.

## The Church-floor

Mark you the floor? that square and speckled stone,
            Which looks so firm and strong,
                Is *Patience*:

And th' other black and grave, wherewith each one
            Is checker'd all along,
                *Humility*:

The gentle rising, which on either hand
            Leads to the choir above,
                Is *Confidence*:

But the sweet cement, which in one sure band
Ties the whole frame, is *Love*
And *Charity*.

Hither sometimes Sin steals, and stains
The marble's neat and curious veins:
But all is cleansed when the marble weeps.
Sometimes Death, puffing at the door,
Blows all the dust about the floor:
But while he thinks to spoil the room, he sweeps.
Blest be the *Architect*, whose art
Could build so strong in a weak heart.

# The Windows

Lord, how can man preach thy eternal word?
He is a brittle crazy glass:
Yet in thy temple thou dost him afford
This glorious and transcendent place,
To be a window, through thy grace.

But when thou dost anneal in glass thy story,
Making thy life to shine within
The holy preachers, then the light and glory
More rev'rend grows, and more doth win:
Which else shows wat'rish, bleak, and thin.

Doctrine and life, colours and light, in one
When they combine and mingle, bring
A strong regard and awe: but speech alone
Doth vanish like a flaring thing,
And in the ear, not conscience ring.

# The Quiddity

My God, a verse is not a crown,
No point of honour, or gay suit,
No hawk, or banquet, or renown,
Nor a good sword, nor yet a lute:

It cannot vault, or dance, or play;
It never was in *France* or *Spain*;
Nor can it entertain the day
With a great stable or demesne:

It is no office, art, or news,
Nor the Exchange, or busy Hall;
But it is that which while I use
I am with thee, and *Most take all*.

# Avarice

Money, thou bane of bliss, and source of woe,
    Whence com'st thou, that thou art so fresh and fine?
    I know thy parentage is base and low:
Man found thee poor and dirty in a mine.
Surely thou didst so little contribute
    To this great kingdom, which thou now hast got,
    That he was fain, when thou wert destitute,
To dig thee out of thy dark cave and grot:
Then forcing thee by fire he made thee bright:
    Nay, thou hast got the face of man; for we
    Have with our stamp and seal transferr'd our right:
Thou art the man, and man but dross to thee.
    Man calleth thee his wealth, who made thee rich;
    And while he digs out thee, falls in the ditch.

# Ana-{ MARY / ARMY }gram

How well her name an *Army* doth present,
In whom the *Lord of Hosts* did pitch his tent!

## To All Angels and Saints

Oh glorious spirits, who after all your bands
See the smooth face of God, without a frown
                  Or strict commands,
Where ev'ryone is king, and hath his crown,
If not upon his head, yet in his hands:

Not out of envy or maliciousness
Do I forbear to crave your special aid:
                  I would address
My vows to thee most gladly, Blessed Maid,
And Mother of my God, in my distress.

Thou art the holy mine, whence came the gold,
The great restorative for all decay
                  In young and old;
Thou art the cabinet where the jewel lay:
Chiefly to thee would I my soul unfold:

But now (alas!) I dare not; for our King,
Whom we do all jointly adore and praise,
                  Bids no such thing:
And where his pleasure no injunction lays
('Tis your own case), ye never move a wing.

All worship is prerogative, and a flower
Of his rich crown, from whom lies no appeal
                  At the last hour:

Therefore we dare not from his garland steal,
To make a posy for inferior power.

Although then others court you, if ye know
What's done on earth, we shall not fare the worse,
                    Who do not so;
Since we are ever ready to disburse,
If anyone our Master's hand can show.


# Employment (II)


He that is weary, let him sit.
                    My soul would stir
And trade in courtesies and wit,
                    Quitting the fur
To cold complexions needing it.

Man is no star, but a quick coal
                    Of mortal fire:
Who blows it not, nor doth control
                    A faint desire,
Lets his own ashes choke his soul.

When th' elements did for place contest
                    With him, whose will
Ordain'd the highest to be best,
                    The earth sat still,
And by the others is opprest.

Life is a business, not good cheer;
                    Ever in wars.
The sun still shineth there or here,
                    Whereas the stars
Watch an advantage to appear.

Oh that I were an orange-tree,
                    That busy plant!
Then should I ever laden be,
                    And never want
Some fruit for him that dressed me.

But we are still too young or old;
                    The man is gone,
Before we do our wares unfold:
                    So we freeze on,
Until the grave increase our cold.

# Denial

When my devotions could not pierce
                    Thy silent ears,
Then was my heart broken, as was my verse:
                    My breast was full of fears
                    And disorder:

My bent thoughts, like a brittle bow,
                    Did fly asunder:
Each took his way; some would to pleasures go,
                    Some to the wars and thunder
                    Of alarms.

As good go anywhere, they say,
                    As to benumb
Both knees and heart, in crying night and day,
                    *Come, come, my God, O come,*
                    But no hearing.

O that thou shouldst give dust a tongue
                    To cry to thee,
And then not hear it crying! all day long
                    My heart was in my knee,
                    But no hearing.

Therefore my soul lay out of sight,
  Untun'd, unstrung:
My feeble spirit, unable to look right,
  Like a nipped blossom, hung
    Discontented.

O cheer and tune my heartless breast,
  Defer no time;
That so thy favours granting my request,
  They and my mind may chime,
    And mend my rhyme.

# Christmas

All after pleasures as I rode one day,
 My horse and I, both tir'd, body and mind,
 With full cry of affections, quite astray,
I took up in the next inn I could find.
There when I came, whom found I but my dear,
 My dearest Lord, expecting till the grief
 Of pleasures brought me to him, ready there
To be all passengers' most sweet relief?
O Thou, whose glorious, yet contracted light,
 Wrapped in night's mantle, stole into a manger,
 Since my dark soul and brutish is thy right,
To man of all beasts be not thou a stranger:
 Furnish and deck my soul, that thou mayst have
 A better lodging than a rack or grave.

The shepherds sing; and shall I silent be?
    My God, no hymn for thee?
My soul's a shepherd too; a flock it feeds
    Of thoughts, and words, and deeds.
The pasture is thy word: the streams, thy grace
    Enriching all the place.
Shepherd and flock shall sing, and all my powers

Out-sing the daylight hours.
Then we will chide the sun for letting night
Take up his place and right:
We sing one common Lord; wherefore he should
Himself the candle hold.
I will go searching, till I find a sun
Shall stay, till we have done;
A willing shiner, that shall shine as gladly,
As frost-nipped suns look sadly.
Then we will sing, and shine all our own day,
And one another pay:
His beams shall cheer my breast, and both so twine,
Till ev'n his beams sing, and my music shine.


## Sighs and Groans


O do not use me
After my sins! look not on my desert,
But on thy glory! then thou wilt reform
And not refuse me: for thou only art
The mighty God, but I a silly worm;
O do not bruise me!

O do not urge me!
For what account can thy ill steward make?
I have abus'd thy stock, destroy'd thy woods,
Suck'd all thy magazines: my head did ache,
Till it found out how to consume thy goods:
O do not scourge me!

O do not blind me!
I have deserv'd that an Egyptian night
Should thicken all my powers, because my lust
Hath still sow'd fig-leaves to exclude thy light:
But I am frailty, and already dust;
O do not grind me!

O do not fill me
With the turn'd vial of thy bitter wrath!
For thou hast other vessels full of blood,
A part whereof my Saviour empti'd hath,
Ev'n unto death: since he di'd for my good,
O do not kill me!

But O reprieve me!
For thou hast life and death at thy command.
Thou art both *Judge* and *Saviour*, *feast* and *rod*,
*Cordial* and *corrosive*: put not thy hand
Into the bitter box; but O my God,
My God, relieve me!

# Vanity

The fleet Astronomer can bore,
And thread the spheres with his quick-piercing mind:
He views their stations, walks from door to door,
Surveys, as if he had design'd
To make a purchase there: he sees their dances,
And knoweth long before
Both their full-ey'd aspects, and secret glances.

The nimble Diver with his side
Cuts through the working waves, that he may fetch
His dearly-earned pearl, which God did hide
On purpose from the vent'rous wretch,
That he might save his life, and also hers,
Who with excessive pride
Her own destruction and his danger wears.

The subtle Chymick can divest
And strip the creature naked, till he find
The callow principles within their nest:
There he imparts to them his mind,

Admitted to their bedchamber, before
                    They appear trim and drest
To ordinary suitors at the door.

                    What hath not man sought out and found,
But his dear God? who yet his glorious law
Embosoms in us, mellowing the ground
                    With showers and frosts, with love and awe,
So that we need not say, Where's this command?
                    Poor man, thou searchest round
To find out *death*, but missest *life* at hand.


# Virtue


Sweet day, so cool, so calm, so bright,
The bridal of the earth and sky:
The dew shall weep thy fall tonight;
                    For thou must die.

Sweet rose, whose hue angry and brave
Bids the rash gazer wipe his eye:
Thy root is ever in its grave,
                    And thou must die.

Sweet spring, full of sweet days and roses,
A box where sweets compacted lie:
My music shows ye have your closes,
                    And all must die.

Only a sweet and virtuous soul,
Like season'd timber, never gives;
But though the whole world turn to coal,
                    Then chiefly lives.

# The Pearl (Matthew 13)

I know the ways of Learning; both the head
And pipes that feed the press, and make it run;
What reason hath from nature borrowed,
Or of itself, like a good housewife, spun
In laws and policy; what the stars conspire,
What willing nature speaks, what forc'd by fire;
Both th' old discoveries, and the new-found seas,
The stock and surplus, cause and history:
All these stand open, or I have the keys:
     Yet I love thee.

I know the ways of Honour, what maintains
The quick returns of courtesy and wit:
In vies of favours whether party gains,
When glory swells the heart, and mouldeth it
To all expressions both of hand and eye,
Which on the world a true-love-knot may tie,
And bear the bundle, wheresoe'er it goes:
How many drams of spirit there must be
To sell my life unto my friends or foes:
     Yet I love thee.

I know the ways of Pleasure, the sweet strains,
The lullings and the relishes of it;
The propositions of hot blood and brains;
What mirth and music mean; what love and wit
Have done these twenty hundred years, and more:
I know the projects of unbridled store:
My stuff is flesh, not brass; my senses live,
And grumble oft, that they have more in me
Than he that curbs them, being but one to five:
     Yet I love thee.

I know all these, and have them in my hand:
Therefore not sealed, but with open eyes
I fly to thee, and fully understand

Both the main sale, and the commodities,
And at what rate and price I have thy love;
With all the circumstances that may move:
Yet through these labyrinths, not my grovelling wit,
But thy silk twist let down from heav'n to me,
Did both conduct and teach me, how by it
        To climb to thee.

# Affliction (II)

Broken in pieces all asunder,
        Lord, hunt me not,
        A thing forgot,
Once a poor creature, now a wonder,
        A wonder tortur'd in the space
        Betwixt this world and that of grace.

My thoughts are all a case of knives,
        Wounding my heart
        With scatter'd smart,
As wat'ring pots give flowers their lives.
        Nothing their fury can control,
        While they do wound and prick my soul.

All my attendants are at strife,
        Quitting their place
        Unto my face:
Nothing performs the task of life:
        The elements are let loose to fight,
        And while I live, try out their right.

Oh help, my God! let not their plot
        Kill them and me,
        And also thee,
Who art my life: dissolve the knot,

As the sun scatters by his light
All the rebellions of the night.

Then shall those powers, which work for grief,
Enter thy pay,
And day by day
Labour thy praise, and my relief;
With care and courage building me,
Till I reach heav'n, and much more, thee.

# Unkindness

Lord, make me coy and tender to offend:
In friendship, first I think, if that agree,
Which I intend,
Unto my friend's intent and end.
I would not use a friend, as I use Thee.

If any touch my friend, or his good name,
It is my honour and my love to free
His blasted fame
From the least spot or thought of blame.
I could not use a friend, as I use Thee.

My friend may spit upon my curious floor:
Would he have gold? I lend it instantly;
But let the poor,
And thou within them, starve at door.
I cannot use a friend, as I use Thee.

When that my friend pretendeth to a place,
I quit my interest, and leave it free:
But when thy grace
Sues for my heart, I thee displace,
Nor would I use a friend, as I use Thee.

Yet can a friend what thou hast done fulfil?
O write in brass, *My God upon a tree*
                       *His blood did spill*
               *Only to purchase my good-will.*
Yet use I not my foes, as I use Thee.

# Life

I made a posy, while the day ran by:
Here will I smell my remnant out, and tie
                My life within this band.
But Time did beckon to the flowers, and they
By noon most cunningly did steal away,
                   And wither'd in my hand.

My hand was next to them, and then my heart:
I took, without more thinking, in good part
                Time's gentle admonition:
Who did so sweetly death's sad taste convey,
Making my mind to smell my fatal day;
                  Yet sug'ring the suspicion.

Farewell dear flowers, sweetly your time ye spent,
Fit, while ye liv'd, for smell or ornament,
                And after death for cures.
I follow straight without complaints or grief,
Since if my scent be good, I care not if
                It be as short as yours.

# Submission

But that thou art my wisdom, Lord,
   And both mine eyes are thine,
My mind would be extremely stirr'd
   For missing my design.

Were it not better to bestow
   Some place and power on me?
Then should thy praises with me grow,
   And share in my degree.

But when I thus dispute and grieve,
   I do resume my sight,
And pilf'ring what I once did give,
   Disseize thee of thy right.

How know I, if thou shouldst me raise,
   That I should then raise thee?
Perhaps great places and thy praise
   Do not so well agree.

Wherefore unto my gift I stand;
   I will no more advise:
Only do thou lend me a hand,
   Since thou hast both mine eyes.

# Justice (I)

I cannot skill of these thy ways.
*Lord, thou didst make me, yet thou woundest me:*
*Lord, thou dost wound me, yet thou dost relieve me:*
*Lord, thou relievest, yet I die by thee:*
*Lord, thou dost kill me, yet thou dost reprieve me.*

But when I mark my life and praise,
    Thy justice me most fitly pays:
For, *I do praise thee, yet I praise thee not:*
*My prayers mean thee, yet my prayers stray:*
*I would do well, yet sin the hand hath got:*
*My soul doth love thee, yet it loves delay.*
    I cannot skill of these my ways.

# Charms and Knots

Who read a chapter when they rise,
Shall ne'er be troubled with ill eyes.

A poor man's rod, when thou dost ride,
Is both a weapon and a guide.

Who shuts his hand, hath lost his gold:
Who opens it, hath it twice told.

Who goes to bed and does not pray,
Maketh two nights to ev'ry day.

Who by aspersions throw a stone
At th' head of others, hit their own.

Who looks on ground with humble eyes,
Finds himself there, and seeks to rise.

When th' hair is sweet through pride or lust,
The powder doth forget the dust.

Take one from ten, and what remains?
Ten still, if sermons go for gains.

In shallow waters heav'n doth show;
But who drinks on, to hell may go.

# Mortification

How soon doth man decay!
When clothes are taken from a chest of sweets
To swaddle infants, whose young breath
Scarce knows the way:
Those clouts are little winding sheets,
Which do consign and send them unto death.

When boys go first to bed,
They step into their voluntary graves,
Sleep binds them fast; only their breath
Makes them not dead:
Successive nights, like rolling waves,
Convey them quickly, who are bound for death.

When youth is frank and free,
And calls for music, while his veins do swell,
All day exchanging mirth and breath
In company:
That music summons to the knell,
Which shall befriend him at the hour of death.

When man grows staid and wise,
Getting a house and home, where he may move

Within the circle of his breath,
Schooling his eyes:
That dumb enclosure maketh love
Unto the coffin, that attends his death.

When age grows low and weak,
Marking his grave, and thawing ev'ry year,
Till all do melt, and drown his breath
When he would speak:
A chair or litter shows the bier,
Which shall convey him to the house of death.

Man, ere he is aware,
Hath put together a solemnity,
And dress'd his hearse, while he has breath
As yet to spare:
Yet Lord, instruct us so to die,
That all these dyings may be life in death.

# Jordan (II)

When first my lines of heav'nly joys made mention,
Such was their lustre, they did so excel,
That I sought out quaint words, and trim invention;
My thoughts began to burnish, sprout, and swell,
Curling with metaphors a plain intention,
Decking the sense, as if it were to sell.

Thousands of notions in my brain did run,
Off'ring their service, if I were not sped:
I often blotted what I had begun;
This was not quick enough, and that was dead.
Nothing could seem too rich to clothe the sun,
Much less those joys which trample on his head.

As flames do work and wind, when they ascend,
So did I weave myself into the sense.
But while I bustled, I might hear a friend
Whisper, *How wide is all this long pretence!*
*There is in love a sweetness ready penn'd:*
*Copy out only that, and save expense.*

# Prayer (II)

Of what an easy quick access,
My blessed Lord, art thou! how suddenly
    May our requests thine ear invade!
To show that state dislikes not easiness,
If I but lift mine eyes, my suit is made:
Thou canst no more not hear, than thou canst die.

Of what supreme almighty power
Is thy great arm, which spans the east and west,
    And tacks the centre to the sphere!
By it do all things live their measur'd hour:
We cannot ask the thing, which is not there,
Blaming the shallowness of our request.

Of what unmeasurable love
Art thou possess'd, who, when thou couldst not die,
    Wert fain to take our flesh and curse,
And for our sakes in person sin reprove,
That by destroying that which ti'd thy purse,
Thou might'st make way for liberality!

Since then these three wait on thy throne,
*Ease, Power,* and *Love*; I value prayer so,
    That were I to leave all but one,
Wealth, fame, endowments, virtues, all should go;
I and dear prayer would together dwell,
And quickly gain, for each inch lost, an ell.

# Sion

Lord, with what glory wast thou serv'd of old,
When Solomon's temple stood and flourished!
　　Where most things were of purest gold;
　　The wood was all embellished
With flowers and carvings, mystical and rare:
All show'd the builders' crav'd the seers' care.

Yet all this glory, all this pomp and state
Did not affect thee much, was not thy aim;
　　Something there was, that sow'd debate:
　　Wherefore thou quitt'st thy ancient claim:
And now thy architecture meets with sin;
For all thy frame and fabric is within.

There thou art struggling with a peevish heart,
Which sometimes crosseth thee, thou sometimes it:
　　The fight is hard on either part.
　　Great God doth fight, he doth submit.
All Solomon's sea of brass and world of stone
Is not so dear to thee as one good groan.

And truly brass and stones are heavy things,
Tombs for the dead, not temples fit for thee:
　　But groans are quick, and full of wings,
　　And all their motions upward be;
And ever as they mount, like larks they sing;
The note is sad, yet music for a King.

# The Quip

The merry world did on a day
With his train-bands and mates agree
To meet together, where I lay,
And all in sport to jeer at me.

First, Beauty crept into a rose,
Which when I pluck'd not, Sir, said she,
Tell me, I pray, Whose hands are those?
*But thou shalt answer, Lord, for me.*

Then Money came, and chinking still,
What tune is this, poor man? said he:
I heard in music you had skill.
*But thou shalt answer, Lord, for me.*

Then came brave Glory puffing by
In silks that whistled, who but he?
He scarce allow'd me half an eye.
*But thou shalt answer, Lord, for me.*

Then came quick Wit and Conversation,
And he would needs a comfort be,
And, to be short, make an oration.
*But thou shalt answer, Lord, for me.*

Yet when the hour of thy design
To answer these fine things shall come,
Speak not at large; say, I am thine:
And then they have their answer home.

# The Dawning

Awake sad heart, whom sorrow ever drowns;
   Take up thine eyes, which feed on earth;
Unfold thy forehead gather'd into frowns:
   Thy Saviour comes, and with him mirth:
                    Awake, awake;
And with a thankful heart his comforts take.
   But thou dost still lament, and pine, and cry;
   And feel his death, but not his victory.

Arise sad heart; if thou do not withstand,
   Christ's resurrection thine may be:
Do not by hanging down break from the hand,
   Which as it riseth, raiseth thee:
                    Arise, arise;
And with his burial-linen dry thine eyes:
   Christ left his grave-clothes, that we might, when grief
   Draws tears, or blood, not want a handkerchief.

# JESU

JESU is in my heart, his sacred name
Is deeply carved there: but th' other week
A great affliction broke the little frame,
Ev'n all to pieces: which I went to seek:
And first I found the corner, where was *J*,
After, where *ES*, and next where *U* was graved.
When I had got these parcels, instantly
I sat me down to spell them, and perceived
That to my broken heart he was *I ease you*,
          And to my whole is *JESU*.

# Business

Canst be idle? canst thou play,
Foolish soul who sinned today?

Rivers run, and springs each one
Know their home, and get them gone:
Hast thou tears, or hast thou none?

If, poor soul, thou hast no tears,
Would thou hadst no faults or fears!
Who hath these, those ill forbears.

Winds still work: it is their plot,
Be the season cold, or hot:
Hast thou sighs, or hast thou not?

If thou hast no sighs or groans,
Would thou hadst no flesh and bones!
Lesser pains 'scape greater ones.

But if yet thou idle be,
Foolish soul, Who di'd for thee?

Who did leave his Father's throne,
To assume thy flesh and bone;
Had he life, or had he none?

If he had not liv'd for thee,
Thou hadst di'd most wretchedly;
And two deaths had been thy fee.

He so far thy good did plot,
That his own self he forgot.
Did he die, or did he not?

If he had not di'd for thee,
Thou hadst liv'd in misery.
Two lives worse than ten deaths be.

And hath any space of breath
'Twixt his sins and Saviour's death?

He that loseth gold, though dross,
Tells to all he meets, his cross:
He that sins, hath he no loss?

He that finds a silver vein,
Thinks on it, and thinks again:
Brings thy Saviour's death no gain?

Who in heart not ever kneels,
Neither sin nor Saviour feels.

# Dialogue

Sweetest Saviour, if my soul
    Were but worth the having,
Quickly should I then control
    Any thought of waiving.
But when all my care and pains
Cannot give the name of gains
To thy wretch so full of stains,
What delight or hope remains?

*What, child, is the balance thine,*
    *Thine the poise and measure?*
*If I say, Thou shalt be mine,*
    *Finger not my treasure.*
*What the gains in having thee*
*Do amount to, only he,*
*Who for man was sold, can see;*
*That transferr'd th' accounts to me.*

But as I can see no merit,
    Leading to this favour:

So the way to fit me for it
    Is beyond my savour.
As the reason then is thine,
So the way is none of mine:
I disclaim the whole design:
Sin disclaims and I resign.

*That is all, if that I could*
    *Get without repining;*
*And my clay, my creature, would*
    *Follow my resigning:*
*That as I did freely part*
*With my glory and desert,*
*Left all joys to feel all smart —*
    Ah! no more: thou break'st my heart.

# Dullness

Why do I languish thus, drooping and dull,
    As if I were all earth?
O give me quickness, that I may with mirth
    Praise thee brim-full!

The wanton lover in a curious strain
    Can praise his fairest fair;
And with quaint metaphors her curled hair
    Curl o'er again.

Thou art my loveliness, my life, my light,
    Beauty alone to me:
Thy bloody death and undeserv'd, makes thee
    Pure red and white.

When all perfections as but one appear,
   That those thy form doth show,
The very dust, where thou dost tread and go,
   Makes beauties here.

Where are my lines then? my approaches? views?
   Where are my window-songs?
Lovers are still pretending, and ev'n wrongs
   Sharpen their Muse:

But I am lost in flesh, whose sugar'd lies

   Still mock me, and grow bold:
Sure thou didst put a mind there, if I could
   Find where it lies.

Lord, clear thy gift, that with a constant wit
   I may but look towards thee:
*Look* only; for to *love* thee, who can be,
   What angel fit?

## Love-joy

As on a window late I cast mine eye,
I saw a vine drop grapes with *J* and *C*
Anneal'd on every bunch. One standing by
Ask'd what it meant. I, who am never loath
To spend my judgement, said, It seem'd to me
To be the body and the letters both
Of *Joy* and *Charity*. Sir, you have not miss'd,
The man replied: It figures *JESUS CHRIST*.

# Hope

I gave to Hope a watch of mine: but he
        An anchor gave to me.
Then an old prayer-book I did present:
        And he an optic sent.
With that I gave a vial full of tears:
        But he a few green ears.
Ah loiterer! I'll no more, no more I'll bring:
        I did expect a ring.

# Time

Meeting with Time, Slack thing, said I,
Thy scythe is dull; whet it for shame.
No marvel, Sir, he did reply,
If it at length deserve some blame:
    But where one man would have me grind it,
    Twenty for one too sharp do find it.

Perhaps some such of old did pass,
Who above all things lov'd this life,
To whom thy scythe a hatchet was,
Which now is but a pruning-knife.
    Christ's coming hath made man thy debter,
    Since by thy cutting he grows better.

And in his blessing thou art blest:
For where thou only wert before
An executioner at best,
Thou art a gard'ner now, and more,
    An usher to convey our souls
    Beyond the utmost stars and poles.

And this is that makes life so long,
While it detains us from our God.
Ev'n pleasures here increase the wrong,
And length of days lengthen the rod.
    Who wants the place, where God doth dwell,
    Partakes already half of hell.

Of what strange length must that needs be,
Which ev'n eternity excludes!
Thus far Time heard me patiently;
Then chafing said, This man deludes:
    What do I here before his door?
    He doth not crave less time, but more.

# Gratefulness

Thou that hast giv'n so much to me,
Give one thing more, a grateful heart.
See how thy beggar works on thee
        By art.

He makes thy gifts occasion more,
And says, If he in this be crosst,
All thou hast giv'n him heretofore
        Is lost.

But thou didst reckon, when at first
Thy word our hearts and hands did crave,
What it would come to at the worst
        To save.

Perpetual knockings at thy door,
Tears sullying thy transparent rooms,
Gift upon gift, much would have more,
        And comes.

This notwithstanding, thou wentst on,
And didst allow us all our noise:
Nay, thou hast made a sigh and groan
              Thy joys.

Not that thou hast not still above
Much better tunes, than groans can make;
But that these country-airs thy love
              Did take.

Wherefore I cry, and cry again;
And in no quiet canst thou be,
Till I a thankful heart obtain
              Of thee:

Not thankful, when it pleaseth me,
As if thy blessings had spare days:
But such a heart, whose pulse may be
              Thy praise.

## Peace

Sweet Peace, where dost thou dwell? I humbly crave,
              Let me once know.
    I sought thee in a secret cave,
      And ask'd, if Peace were there.
A hollow wind did seem to answer, No;
              Go seek elsewhere.

I did; and going did a rainbow note:
              Surely, thought I,
    This is the lace of Peace's coat:
      I will search out the matter.
But while I look'd, the clouds immediately
              Did break and scatter.

Then went I to a garden, and did spy
                                A gallant flower,
        The crown imperial: Sure, said I,
            Peace at the root must dwell.
But when I digg'd, I saw a worm devour
                                What show'd so well.


At length I met a rev'rend good old man,
                                Whom when for Peace
        I did demand, he thus began:
            There was a Prince of old
At Salem dwelt, who liv'd with good increase
                                Of flock and fold.


He sweetly liv'd; yet sweetness did not save
                                His life from foes.
        But after death out of his grave
            There sprang twelve stalks of wheat:
Which many wond'ring at, got some of those
                                To plant and set.


It prosper'd strangely, and did soon disperse
                                Through all the earth:
        For they that taste it do rehearse,
            That virtue lies therein,
A secret virtue bringing peace and mirth
                                By flight of sin.


Take of this grain, which in my garden grows,
                                And grows for you;
        Make bread of it: and that repose
            And peace, which ev'rywhere
With so much earnestness you do pursue,
                                Is only there.

# Confession

O what a cunning guest
Is this same grief! Within my heart I made
   Closets; and in them many a chest;
   And, like a master in my trade,
In those chests, boxes; in each box, a till:
Yet grief knows all, and enters when he will.

   No screw, no piercer can
Into a piece of timber work and wind,
   As God's afflictions into man,
   When he a torture hath design'd.
They are too subtle for the subtlest hearts;
And fall, like rheums, upon the tend'rest parts.

   We are the earth; and they,
Like moles within us, heave, and cast about:
   And till they foot and clutch their prey,
   They never cool, much less give out.
No smith can make such locks, but they have keys:
Closets are halls to them; and hearts, high-ways.

   Only an open breast
Doth shut them out, so that they cannot enter;
   Or, if they enter, cannot rest,
   But quickly seek some new adventure.
Smooth open hearts no fast'ning have; but fiction
Doth give a hold and handle to affliction.

   Wherefore my faults and sins,
Lord, I acknowledge; take thy plagues away:
   For since confession pardon wins,
   I challenge here the brightest day,
The clearest diamond: let them do their best,
They shall be thick and cloudy to my breast.

# Giddiness

Oh, what a thing is man! how far from power,
      From settled peace and rest!
He is some twenty sev'ral men at least
      Each sev'ral hour.

One while he counts of heav'n, as of his treasure:
      But then a thought creeps in,
And calls him coward, who for fear of sin
      Will lose a pleasure.

Now he will fight it out, and to the wars;
      Now eat his bread in peace,
And snudge in quiet: now he scorns increase;
      Now all day spares.

He builds a house, which quickly down must go,
      As if a whirlwind blew
And crush'd the building: and it's partly true,
      His mind is so.

O what a sight were man, if his attires
      Did alter with his mind;
And like a dolphin's skin, his clothes combin'd
      With his desires!

Surely if each one saw another's heart,
      There would be no commerce,
No sale or bargain pass: all would disperse,
      And live apart.

Lord, mend or rather make us: one creation
      Will not suffice our turn:
Except thou make us daily, we shall spurn
      Our own salvation.

# The Bunch of Grapes

Joy, I did lock thee up: but some bad man
           Hath let thee out again:
And now, methinks, I am where I began
           Sev'n years ago: one vogue and vein,
           One air of thoughts usurps my brain.
I did towards Canaan draw; but now I am
Brought back to the Red Sea, the sea of shame.

For as the Jews of old by God's command
           Travell'd, and saw no town,
So now each Christian hath his journeys spann'd:
           Their story pens and sets us down.
           A single deed is small renown.
God's works are wide, and let in future times;
His ancient justice overflows our crimes.

Then have we too our guardian fires and clouds;
           Our Scripture-dew drops fast:
We have our sands and serpents, tents and shrouds;
           Alas! our murmurings come not last.
           But where's the cluster? where's the taste
Of mine inheritance? Lord, if I must borrow,
Let me as well take up their joy, as sorrow.

But can he want the grape, who hath the wine?
           I have their fruit and more.
Blessed be God, who prosper'd *Noah*'s vine,
           And made it bring forth grapes' good store.
           But much more him I must adore,
Who of the Law's sour juice sweet wine did make,
Ev'n God himself being pressed for my sake.

# Man's Medley

Hark, how the birds do sing,
        And woods do ring.
All creatures have their joy: and man hath his.
        Yet if we rightly measure,
            Man's joy and pleasure
Rather hereafter, than in present, is.

To this life things of sense
        Make their pretence:
In th' other angels have a right by birth:
        Man ties them both alone,
            And makes them one,
With th' one hand touching heav'n, with th' other earth.

In soul he mounts and flies,
        In flesh he dies.
He wears a stuff whose thread is coarse and round,
        But trimm'd with curious lace,
            And should take place
After the trimming, not the stuff and ground.

Not that he may not here
        Taste of the cheer,
But as birds drink, and straight lift up their head,
        So he must sip and think
            Of better drink
He may attain to, after he is dead.

But as his joys are double,
        So is his trouble.
He hath two winters, other things but one:
        Both frosts and thoughts do nip,
            And bite his lip;
And he of all things fears two deaths alone.

Yet ev'n the greatest griefs
     May be reliefs,
Could he but take them right, and in their ways.
     Happy is he, whose heart
     Hath found the art
To turn his double pains to double praise.

# The Storm

If as the winds and waters here below
     Do fly and flow,
My sighs and tears as busy were above,
     Sure they would move
And much effect thee, as tempestuous times
Amaze poor mortals, and object their crimes.

Stars have their storms, ev'n in a high degree,
     As well as we.
A throbbing conscience spurred by remorse
     Hath a strange force:
It quits the earth, and mounting more and more
Dares to assault thee, and besiege thy door.

There it stands knocking, to thy music's wrong,
     And drowns the song.
Glory and honour are set by, till it
     An answer get.
Poets have wrong'd poor storms: such days are best;
They purge the air without, within the breast.

# Artillery

As I one ev'ning sat before my cell,
Methoughts a star did shoot into my lap.
I rose, and shook my clothes, as knowing well,
That from small fires comes oft no small mishap.
    When suddenly I heard one say,
     *Do as thou usest, disobey,*
     *Expel good motions from thy breast,*
*Which have the face of fire, but end in rest.*

I, who had heard of music in the spheres,
But not of speech in stars, began to muse:
But turning to my God, whose ministers
The stars and all things are: If I refuse,
    Dread Lord, said I, so oft my good,
    Then I refuse not ev'n with blood
    To wash away my stubborn thought:
For I will do or suffer what I ought,

But I have stars and shooters too,
Born where thy servants both artilleries use.
My tears and prayers night and day do woo,
And work up to thee; yet thou dost refuse.
    Not but I am (I must say still)
    Much more oblig'd to do thy will,
    Than thou to grant mine: but because
Thy promise now hath ev'n set thee thy laws.

Then we are shooters both, and thou dost deign
To enter combat with us, and contest
With thine own clay. But I would parley fain:
Shun not my arrows, and behold my breast.
    Yet if thou shunnest, I am thine:
    I must be so, if I am mine.
    There is no articling with thee:
I am but finite, yet thine infinitely.

# Justice (II)

O dreadful Justice, what a fright and terror
          Wast thou of old,
          When sin and error
      Did show and shape thy looks to me,
      And through their glass discolour thee!
He that did but look up, was proud and bold.

The dishes of thy balance seem'd to gape,
          Like two great pits;
          The beam and scape
      Did like some torturing engine show;
      Thy hand above did burn and glow,
Daunting the stoutest hearts, the proudest wits.

But now that Christ's pure veil presents the sight,
          I see no fears:
          Thy hand is white,
      Thy scales like buckets, which attend
      And interchangeably descend,
Lifting to heaven from this well of tears.

For where before thou still didst call on me,
          Now I still touch
          And harp on thee.
      God's promises have made thee mine;
      Why should I justice now decline?
Against me there is none, but for me much.

# The Pilgrimage

I travell'd on, seeing the hill, where lay
            My expectation.
      A long it was and weary way.
            The gloomy cave of Desperation
I left on th' one, and on the other side
            The rock of Pride.

And so I came to Fancy's meadow strow'd
            With many a flower:
      Fain would I here have made abode,
      But I was quicken'd by my hour.
So to Care's copse I came, and there got through
            With much ado.

That led me to the wild of Passion, which
            Some call the wold;
      A wasted place, but sometimes rich.
      Here I was robb'd of all my gold,
Save one good angel, which a friend had ti'd
            Close to my side.

At length I got unto the gladsome hill,
            Where lay my hope,
      Where lay my heart; and climbing still,
      When I had gain'd the brow and top,
A lake of brackish waters on the ground
            Was all I found.

With that abash'd and struck with many a sting
            Of swarming fears,
      I fell, and cri'd, Alas my King!
      Can both the way and end be tears?
Yet taking heart I rose, and then perceiv'd
            I was deceiv'd:

My hill was further: so I flung away,
            Yet heard a cry

Just as I went, *None goes that way*
*And lives*: If that be all, said I,
After so foul a journey death is fair,
And but a chair.

## The Holdfast

I threaten'd to observe the strict decree
    Of my dear God with all my power and might.
    But I was told by one, it could not be;
Yet I might trust in God to be my light.
Then will I trust, said I, in him alone.
    Nay, ev'n to trust in him, was also his:
    We must confess that nothing is our own.
Then I confess that he my succour is:
But to have nought is ours, not to confess
    That we have nought. I stood amaz'd at this,
    Much troubled, till I heard a friend express,
That all things were more ours by being his.
    What Adam had, and forfeited for all,
    Christ keepeth now, who cannot fail or fall.

## Complaining

Do not beguile my heart,
    Because thou art
My power and wisdom. Put me not to shame,
    Because I am
Thy clay that weeps, thy dust that calls.

Thou art the Lord of glory;
    The deed and story

Are both thy due: but I a silly fly,
        That live or die
According as the weather falls.

Art thou all justice, Lord?
        Shows not thy word
More attributes? Am I all throat or eye,
        To weep or cry?
Have I no parts but those of grief?

Let not thy wrathful power
        Afflict my hour,
My inch of life: or let thy gracious power
        Contract my hour,
That I may climb and find relief.

# The Discharge

Busy enquiring heart, what wouldst thou know?
        Why dost thou pry,
And turn, and leer, and with a lickerous eye
        Look high and low;
And in thy lookings stretch and grow?

Hast thou not made thy counts, and summ'd up all?
        Did not thy heart
Give up the whole, and with the whole depart?
        Let what will fall:
That which is past who can recall?

Thy life is God's, thy time to come is gone,
        And is his right.
He is thy night at noon: he is at night
        Thy noon alone.
The crop is his, for he hath sown.

And well it was for thee, when this befell,
        That God did make
Thy business his, and in thy life partake:
        For thou canst tell,
   If it be his once, all is well.

Only the present is thy part and fee.
        And happy thou,
If, though thou didst not beat thy future brow,
        Thou couldst well see
   What present things requir'd of thee.

They ask enough; why shouldst thou further go?
        Raise not the mud
Of future depths, but drink the clear and good.
        Dig not for woe
   In times to come; for it will grow.

Man and the present fit: if he provide,
        He breaks the square.
This hour is mine: if for the next I care,
        I grow too wide,
   And do encroach upon death's side.

For death each hour environs and surrounds.
        He that would know
And care for future chances, cannot go
        Unto those grounds,
   But through a churchyard which them bounds.

Things present shrink and die: but they that spend
        Their thoughts and sense
On future grief, do not remove it thence,
        But it extend,
   And draw the bottom out an end.

God chains the dog till night: wilt loose the chain,
        And wake thy sorrow?
Wilt thou forestall it, and now grieve tomorrow,

And then again
Grieve over freshly all thy pain?

Either grief will not come: or if it must,
Do not forecast.
And while it cometh, it is almost past.
Away distrust:
My God hath promis'd: he is just.

# An Offering

Come, bring thy gift. If blessings were as slow
As men's returns, what would become of fools?
What hast thou there? a heart? but is it pure?
Search well and see; for hearts have many holes.
Yet one pure heart is nothing to bestow:
In Christ two natures met to be thy cure.

O that within us hearts had propagation,
Since many gifts do challenge many hearts!
Yet one, if good, may title to a number;
And single things grow fruitful by deserts.
In public judgements one may be a nation,
And fence a plague, while others sleep and slumber.

But all I fear is lest thy heart displease,
As neither good, nor one: so oft divisions
Thy lusts have made, and not thy lusts alone;
Thy passions also have their set partitions.
These parcel out thy heart: recover these,
And thou mayst offer many gifts in one.

There is a balsam, or indeed a blood,
Dropping from heav'n, which doth both cleanse and close
All sorts of wounds, of such strange force it is.
Seek out this All-heal, and seek no repose,

Until thou find and use it to thy good:
Then bring thy gift, and let thy hymn be this:

> Since my sadness
> Into gladness
> Lord thou dost convert,
> O accept
> What thou hast kept,
> As thy due desert.

> Had I many,
> Had I any
> (For this heart is none),
> All were thine
> And none of mine:
> Surely thine alone.

> Yet thy favour
> May give savour
> To this poor oblation;
> And it raise
> To be thy praise,
> And be my salvation.

# The Bag

Away despair! my gracious Lord doth hear.
  Though winds and waves assault my keel,
  He doth preserve it; he doth steer,
  Ev'n when the boat seems most to reel.
  Storms are the triumph of his art:
Well may he close his eyes, but not his heart.

Hast thou not heard, that my Lord JESUS di'd?
  Then let me tell thee a strange story.
  The God of power, as he did ride

In his majestic robes of glory,
    Resolv'd to light; and so one day
He did descend, undressing all the way.

The stars his tire of light and rings obtain'd,
    The clouds his bow, the fire his spear,
    The sky his azure mantle gain'd.
    And when they ask'd, what he would wear,
    He smil'd and said as he did go,
He had new clothes a-making here below.

When he was come, as travellers are wont,
    He did repair unto an inn.
    Both then, and after, many a brunt
    He did endure to cancel sin:
    And having giv'n the rest before,
Here he gave up his life to pay our score.

But as he was returning, there came one
    That ran upon him with a spear.
    He, who came hither all alone,
    Bringing nor man, nor arms, nor fear,
    Receiv'd the blow upon his side,
And straight he turn'd, and to his brethren cri'd,

If ye have anything to send or write,
    I have no bag, but here is room:
    Unto my Father's hands and sight,
    Believe me, it shall safely come.
    That I shall mind, what you impart,
Look, you may put it very near my heart.

Or if hereafter any of my friends
    Will use me in this kind, the door
    Shall still be open; what he sends
    I will present, and somewhat more,
    Not to his hurt. Sighs will convey
Anything to me. Hark despair, away.

# The Collar

I struck the board, and cri'd, No more.
        I will abroad.
What? shall I ever sigh and pine?
My lines and life are free; free as the road,
      Loose as the wind, as large as store.
        Shall I be still in suit?
Have I no harvest but a thorn
To let me blood, and not restore
What I have lost with cordial fruit?
              Sure there was wine
Before my sighs did dry it: there was corn
      Before my tears did drown it.
    Is the year only lost to me?
      Have I no bays to crown it?
No flowers, no garlands gay? all blasted?
        All wasted?
No so, my heart: but there is fruit,
         And thou hast hands.
Recover all thy sigh-blown age
On double pleasures: leave thy cold dispute
Of what is fit, and not. Forsake thy cage,
        Thy rope of sands,
Which petty thoughts have made, and made to thee
    Good cable, to enforce and draw,
        And be thy law,
While thou didst wink and wouldst not see.
        Away; take heed:
        I will abroad.
Call in thy death's head there: tie up thy fears.
        He that forbears
    To suit and serve his need,
      Deserves his load.
But as I rav'd and grew more fierce and wild
        At every word,
Methoughts I heard one calling, *Child*:
        And I repli'd, *My Lord*.

# The Call

Come, my Way, my Truth, my Life:
Such a Way, as gives us breath:
Such a Truth, as ends all strife:
Such a Life, as killeth death.

Come, my Light, my Feast, my Strength:
Such a Light, as shows a feast:
Such a Feast, as mends in length:
Such a Strength, as makes his guest.

Come, my Joy, my Love, my Heart:
Such a Joy, as none can move:
Such a Love, as none can part:
Such a Heart, as joys in love.

# Clasping of Hands

Lord, thou art mine, and I am thine,
If mine I am: and thine much more,
Than I or ought, or can be mine.
Yet to be thine, doth me restore;
So that again I now am mine,
And with advantage mine the more,
Since this being mine, brings with it thine,
And thou with me dost thee restore.
    If I without thee would be mine,
    I neither should be mine nor thine.

Lord, I am thine, and thou art mine:
So mine thou art, that something more
I may presume thee mine, than thine.
For thou didst suffer to restore
Not thee, but me, and to be mine:

And with advantage mine the more,
Since thou in death wast none of thine,
Yet then as mine didst me restore.
　　O be mine still! still make me thine!
　　Or rather make no Thine and Mine!

# Joseph's Coat

Wounded I sing, tormented I indite,
　Thrown down I fall into a bed, and rest:
Sorrow hath chang'd its note: such is his will,
Who changeth all things, as him pleaseth best.
　For well he knows, if but one grief and smart
Amongst my many had his full career,
Sure it would carry with it ev'n my heart,
And both would run until they found a bier
　To fetch the body; both being due to grief.
But he hath spoil'd the race; and giv'n to anguish
One of Joy's coats, ticing it with relief
To linger in me, and together languish.
　I live to show his power, who once did bring
　My *joys* to *weep*, and now my *griefs* to *sing*.

# The Pulley

　　When God at first made man,
Having a glass of blessings standing by,
Let us (said he) pour on him all we can:
Let the world's riches, which dispersed lie,
　　Contract into a span.

　　So strength first made a way;
Then beauty flow'd, then wisdom, honour, pleasure:

When almost all was out, God made a stay,
Perceiving that alone of all his treasure
     Rest in the bottom lay.

     For if I should (said he)
Bestow this jewel also on my creature.
He would adore my gifts instead of me,
And rest in nature, not the God of nature:
     So both should losers be.

     Yet let him keep the rest,
But keep them with repining restlessness:
Let him be rich and weary, that at least,
If goodness lead him not, yet weariness
     May toss him to my breast.


# Grief


O who will give me tears? Come all ye springs,
Dwell in my head and eyes: come clouds, and rain:
My grief hath need of all the wat'ry things,
That nature hath produc'd. Let ev'ry vein
Suck up a river to supply mine eyes,
My weary weeping eyes, too dry for me,
Unless they get new conduits, new supplies
To bear them out, and with my state agree.
What are two shallow fords, two little spouts
Of a less world? the greater is but small,
A narrow cupboard for my griefs and doubts,
Which want provision in the midst of all.
Verses, ye are too fine a thing, too wise
For my rough sorrows: cease, be dumb and mute,
Give up your feet and running to mine eyes,
And keep your measures for some lover's lute,
Whose grief allows him music and a rhyme:

For mine excludes both measure, tune, and time.
                              Alas, my God!


# The Flower


        How fresh, O Lord, how sweet and clean
Are thy returns! ev'n as the flowers in spring;
        To which, besides their own demean,
The late-past frosts tributes of pleasure bring.
                    Grief melts away
                    Like snow in May,
        As if there were no such cold thing.

        Who would have thought my shrivell'd heart
Could have recover'd greenness? It was gone
        Quite under ground; as flowers depart
To see their mother-root, when they have blown;
                    Where they together
                    All the hard weather,
        Dead to the world, keep house unknown.

        These are thy wonders, Lord of power,
Killing and quick'ning, bringing down to hell
        And up to heaven in an hour;
Making a chiming of a passing-bell.
                    We say amiss,
                    This or that is:
        Thy word is all, if we could spell.

        O that I once past changing were,
Fast in thy Paradise, where no flower can wither!
        Many a spring I shoot up fair,
Off'ring at heav'n, growing and groaning thither:
                    Nor doth my flower
                    Want a spring-shower,
        My sins and I joining together.

But while I grow in a straight line,
Still upwards bent, as if heav'n were mine own,
Thy anger comes, and I decline:
What frost to that? what pole is not the zone,
Where all things burn,
When thou dost turn,
And the least frown of thine is shown?

And now in age I bud again,
After so many deaths I live and write;
I once more smell the dew and rain,
And relish versing: O my only light,
It cannot be
That I am he
On whom thy tempests fell all night.

These are thy wonders, Lord of love,
To make us see we are but flowers that glide:
Which when we once can find and prove,
Thou hast a garden for us, where to bide.
Who would be more,
Swelling through store,
Forfeit their Paradise by their pride.

# Dotage

False glozing pleasures, casks of happiness,
Foolish night-fires, women's and children's wishes,
Chases in arras, gilded emptiness,
Shadows well mounted, dreams in a career,
Embroider'd lies, nothing between two dishes:
These are the pleasures here.

True earnest sorrows, rooted miseries,
Anguish in grain, vexations ripe and blown,

Sure-footed griefs, solid calamities,
Plain demonstrations, evident and clear,
Fetching their proofs ev'n from the very bone:
      These are the sorrows here.

But oh the folly of distracted men,
Who griefs in earnest, joys in jest pursue;
Preferring, like brute beasts, a loathsome den
Before a court, ev'n that above so clear,
Where are no sorrows, but delights more true
      Than miseries are here!

# The Son

Let foreign nations of their language boast,
What fine variety each tongue affords:
I like our language, as our men and coast:
Who cannot dress it well, want wit, not words.
How neatly do we give one only name
To parents' issue and the sun's bright star!
A son is light and fruit; a fruitful flame
Chasing the father's dimness, carri'd far
From the first man in th' East, to fresh and new
Western discov'ries of posterity.
So in one word our Lord's humility
We turn upon him in a sense most true;
   For what Christ once in humbleness began,
   We him in glory call, *The Son of Man*.

# A True Hymn

My joy, my life, my crown!
My heart was meaning all the day,
Somewhat it fain would say:
And still it runneth mutt'ring up and down
With only this, *My joy, my life, my crown.*

Yet slight not these few words:
If truly said, they may take part
Among the best in art.
The fineness which a hymn or psalm affords,
Is, when the soul unto the lines accords.

He who craves all the mind,
And all the soul, and strength, and time,
If the words only rhyme,
Justly complains, that somewhat is behind
To make his verse, or write a hymn in kind.

Whereas if th' heart be moved,
Although the verse be somewhat scant,
God doth supply the want.
As when th' heart says (sighing to be approved)
*O, could I love!* and stops: God writeth, *Loved.*

# A Dialogue-Anthem

Christian. Death.

*Chr*:  Alas, poor Death, where is thy glory?
        Where is thy famous force, thy ancient sting?
*Dea*:  *Alas poor mortal, void of story,*
        *Go spell and read how I have kill'd thy King.*
*Chr*:  Poor Death! and who was hurt thereby?

Thy curse being laid on him, makes thee accurst.

*Dea*:    *Let losers talk: yet thou shalt die;*
      *These arms shall crush thee.*

*Chr*:                     Spare not, do thy worst.
I shall be one day better than before:
Thou so much worse, that thou shalt be no more.

## The Water-course

Thou who dost dwell and linger here below,
Since the condition of this world is frail,
Where of all plants afflictions soonest grow,
If troubles overtake thee, do not wail:

For who can look for less, that loveth $\begin{cases} \text{Life?} \\ \text{Strife?} \end{cases}$

But rather turn the pipe and water's course
To serve thy sins, and furnish thee with store
Of sov'reign tears, springing from true remorse:
That so in pureness thou mayst him adore,

Who gives to man, as he sees fit, $\begin{cases} \text{Salvation.} \\ \text{Damnation.} \end{cases}$

## Bitter-sweet

Ah my dear angry Lord,
Since thou dost love, yet strike,
Cast down, yet help afford,
Sure I will do the like.

I will complain, yet praise;
I will bewail, approve:
And all my sour-sweet days
I will lament, and love.

# The Glance

When first thy sweet and gracious eye
Vouchsaf'd ev'n in the midst of youth and night
To look upon me, who before did lie
    Welt'ring in sin,
  I felt a sugar'd strange delight,
Passing all cordials made by any art,
Bedew, embalm, and overrun my heart,
    And take it in.

Since that time many a bitter storm
My soul hath felt, ev'n able to destroy,
Had the malicious and ill-meaning harm
    His swing and sway:
  But still thy sweet original joy,
Sprung from thine eye, did work within my soul,
And surging griefs, when they grew bold, control,
    And got the day.

If thy first glance so powerful be,
A mirth but open'd and seal'd up again,
What wonders shall we feel, when we shall see
    Thy full-ey'd love!
  When thou shalt look us out of pain,
And one aspect of thine spend in delight
More than a thousand suns disburse in light,
    In heav'n above.

# Mary Magdalene

When blessed Mary wip'd her Saviour's feet
(Whose precepts she had trampled on before),
And wore them for a jewel on her head,
    Showing his steps should be the street,
    Wherein she thenceforth evermore
With pensive humbleness would live and tread:

She being stain'd herself, why did she strive
To make him clean, who could not be defil'd?
Why kept she not her tears for her own faults,
    And not his feet? Though we could dive
    In tears like seas, our sins are pil'd
Deeper than they, in words, and works, and thoughts.

Dear soul, she knew who did vouchsafe and deign
To bear her filth; and that her sins did dash
Ev'n God himself: wherefore she was not loath,
    As she had brought wherewith to stain,
    So to bring in wherewith to wash:
And yet in washing one, she washed both.

# Aaron

Holiness on the head,
    Light and perfections on the breast,
Harmonious bells below, raising the dead
    To lead them unto life and rest:
        Thus are true Aarons drest.

Profaneness in my head,
    Defects and darkness in my breast,
A noise of passions ringing me for dead

Unto a place where is no rest:
    Poor priest thus am I drest.

    Only another head
I have, another heart and breast,
Another music, making live not dead,
    Without whom I could have no rest:
        In him I am well drest.

        Christ is my only head,
    My alone only heart and breast,
My only music, striking me ev'n dead;
    That to the old man I may rest,
        And be in him new drest.

        So holy in my head,
    Perfect and light in my dear breast,
My doctrine tun'd by Christ (who is not dead,
    But lives in me while I do rest),
        Come people; Aaron's drest.


# The Odour (2 Corinthians 2)


How sweetly doth *My Master* sound! *My Master!*
    As ambergris leaves a rich scent
        Unto the taster:
    So do these words a sweet content,
An oriental fragrancy, *My Master*.

With these all day I do perfume my mind,
    My mind ev'n thrust into them both:
        That I might find
    What cordials make this curious broth,
This broth of smells, that feeds and fats my mind.

*My Master*, shall I speak? O that to thee
    *My servant* were a little so,

As flesh may be;
That these two words might creep and grow
To some degree of spiciness to thee!

Then should the pomander, which was before
A speaking sweet, mend by reflection,
And tell me more:
For pardon of my imperfection
Would warm and work it sweeter than before.

For when *My Master*, which alone is sweet,
And ev'n in my unworthiness pleasing,
Shall call and meet,
*My servant*, as thee not displeasing,
That call is but the breathing of the sweet.

This breathing would with gains by sweet'ning me
(As sweet things traffic when they meet)
Return to thee.
And so this new commerce and sweet
Should all my life employ, and busy me.

## The Forerunners

The harbingers are come. See, see their mark:
White is their colour, and behold my head.
But must they have my brain? must they dispark
Those sparkling notions, which therein were bred?
Must dullness turn me to a clod?
Yet have they left me, *Thou art still my God.*

Good men ye be, to leave me my best room,
Ev'n all my heart, and what is lodged there:
I pass not, I, what of the rest become,
So *Thou art still my God*, be out of fear.
He will be pleased with that ditty;
And if I please him, I write fine and witty.

Farewell sweet phrases, lovely metaphors.
But will ye leave me thus? when ye before
Of stews and brothels only knew the doors,
Then did I wash you with my tears, and more,
   Brought you to church well dressed and clad:
My God must have my best, ev'n all I had.

Lovely enchanting language, sugar-cane,
Honey of roses, whither wilt thou fly?
Hath some fond lover tic'd thee to thy bane?
And wilt thou leave the church, and love a sty?
   Fie, thou wilt soil thy broider'd coat,
And hurt thyself, and him that sings the note.

Let foolish lovers, if they will love dung,
With canvas, not with arras, clothe their shame:
Let folly speak in her own native tongue.
True beauty dwells on high: ours is a flame
   But borrow'd thence to light us thither.
Beauty and beauteous words should go together.

Yet if you go, I pass not; take your way:
For, *Thou art still my God*, is all that ye
Perhaps with more embellishment can say.
Go birds of spring: let winter have his fee;
   Let a bleak paleness chalk the door,
So all within be livelier than before.

# The Rose

  Press me not to take more pleasure
   In this world of sugar'd lies,
 And to use a larger measure
   Than my strict, yet welcome size.

First, there is no pleasure here:
    Colour'd griefs indeed there are,
Blushing woes, that look as clear
    As if they could beauty spare.

Or if such deceits there be,
    Such delights I meant to say,
There are no such things to me,
    Who have pass'd my right away.

But I will not much oppose
    Unto what you now advise:
Only take this gentle rose,
    And therein my answer lies.

What is fairer than a rose?
    What is sweeter? yet it purgeth.
Purgings enmity disclose,
    Enmity forbearance urgeth.

If then all that worldlings prize
    Be contracted to a rose,
Sweetly there indeed it lies,
    But it biteth in the close.

So this flower doth judge and sentence
    Worldly joys to be a scourge:
For they all produce repentance,
    And repentance is a purge.

But I health, not physic choose:
    Only though I you oppose,
Say that fairly I refuse,
    For my answer is a rose.

# Discipline

Throw away thy rod,
Throw away thy wrath:
        O my God,
Take the gentle path.

For my heart's desire
Unto thee is bent:
        I aspire
To a full consent.

Not a word or look
I affect to own,
        But by book,
And thy book alone.

Though I fail, I weep:
Though I halt in pace,
        Yet I creep
To the throne of grace.

Then let wrath remove;
Love will do the deed:
        For with love
Stony hearts will bleed.

Love is swift of foot;
Love's a man of war,
        And can shoot,
And can hit from far.

Who can 'scape his bow?
That which wrought on thee,
        Brought thee low,
Needs must work on me.

Throw away thy rod;
Though man frailties hath,

                        Thou art God:
  Throw away thy wrath.


# The Invitation


  Come ye hither all, whose taste
                        Is your waste;
  Save your cost, and mend your fare.
  God is here prepar'd and drest,
                        And the feast,
  God, in whom all dainties are.

  Come ye hither all, whom wine
                        Doth define,
  Naming you not to your good:
  Weep what ye have drunk amiss,
                        And drink this,
  Which before ye drink is blood.

  Come ye hither all, whom pain
                        Doth arraign,
  Bringing all your sins to sight:
  Taste and fear not: God is here
                        In this cheer,
  And on sin doth cast the fright.

  Come ye hither all, whom joy
                        Doth destroy,
  While ye graze without your bounds:
  Here is joy that drowneth quite
                        Your delight,
  As a flood the lower grounds.

  Come ye hither all, whose love
                        Is your dove,
  And exalts you to the sky:

Here is love, which having breath
                          Ev'n in death,
After death can never die.

Lord I have invited all,
                          And I shall
Still invite, still call to thee:
For it seems but just and right
                          In my sight,
Where is all, there all should be.

# The Banquet

Welcome sweet and sacred cheer,
                          Welcome dear;
With me, in me, live and dwell:
For thy neatness passeth sight,
                          Thy delight
Passeth tongue to taste or tell.

O what sweetness from the bowl
                          Fills my soul,
Such as is, and makes divine!
Is some star (fled from the sphere)
                          Melted there,
As we sugar melt in wine?

Or hath sweetness in the bread
                          Made a head
To subdue the smell of sin;
Flowers, and gums, and powders giving
                          All their living,
Lest the enemy should win?

Doubtless, neither star nor flower
                          Hath the power

Such a sweetness to impart:
Only God, who gives perfumes,
                    Flesh assumes,
And with it perfumes my heart.


But as pomanders and wood
                    Still are good,
Yet being bruis'd are better scented,
God, to show how far his love
                    Could improve,
Here, as broken, is presented.


When I had forgot my birth,
                    And on earth
In delights of earth was drown'd,
God took blood, and needs would be
                    Spilt with me,
And so found me on the ground.


Having rais'd me to look up,
                    In a cup
Sweetly he doth meet my taste.
But I still being low and short,
                    Far from court,
Wine becomes a wing at last.


For with it alone I fly
                    To the sky:
Where I wipe mine eyes, and see
What I seek, for what I sue;
                    Him I view,
Who hath done so much for me.


Let the wonder of his pity
                    Be my ditty,
And take up my lines and life:
Hearken under pain of death,
                    Hands and breath;
Strive in this, and love the strife.

# The Posy

Let wits contest,
And with their words and posies windows fill:
*Less than the least*
*Of all thy mercies*, is my posy still.

This on my ring,
This by my picture, in my book I write:
Whether I sing,
Or say, or dictate, this is my delight.

Invention rest,
Comparisons go play, wit use thy will:
*Less than the least*
*Of all God's mercies*, is my posy still.

# The Elixir

Teach me, my God and King,
In all things thee to see,
And what I do in anything,
To do it as for thee:

Not rudely, as a beast,
To run into an action;
But still to make thee prepossest,
And give it his perfection.

A man that looks on glass,
On it may stay his eye;
Or if he pleaseth, through it pass,
And then the heav'n espy.

All may of thee partake:
Nothing can be so mean,
Which with his tincture (for thy sake)
Will not grow bright and clean.

A servant with this clause
Makes drudgery divine:
Who sweeps a room, as for thy laws,
Makes that and th' action fine.

This is the famous stone
That turneth all to gold:
For that which God doth touch and own
Cannot for less be told.

# A Wreath

A wreathed garland of deserved praise,
Of praise deserved, unto thee I give,
I give to thee, who knowest all my ways,
My crooked winding ways, wherein I live,
Wherein I die, not live: for life is straight,
Straight as a line, and ever tends to thee,
To thee, who art more far above deceit,
Than deceit seems above simplicity.
Give me simplicity, that I may live,
So live and like, that I may know, thy ways,
Know them and practise them: then shall I give
For this poor wreath, give thee a crown of praise.

# Death

Death, thou wast once an uncouth hideous thing,
                              Nothing but bones,
            The sad effect of sadder groans:
Thy mouth was open, but thou couldst not sing.

For we consider'd thee as at some six
                              Or ten years hence,
            After the loss of life and sense,
Flesh being turn'd to dust, and bones to sticks.

We look'd on this side of thee, shooting short;
                              Where we did find
            The shells of fledge souls left behind,
Dry dust, which sheds no tears, but may extort.

But since our Saviour's death did put some blood
                              Into thy face,
            Thou art grown fair and full of grace,
Much in request, much sought for as a good.

For we do now behold thee gay and glad,
                              As at doomsday;
            When souls shall wear their new array,
And all thy bones with beauty shall be clad.

Therefore we can go die as sleep, and trust
                              Half that we have
            Unto an honest faithful grave;
Making our pillows either down, or dust.

# Doomsday

Come away,
Make no delay.
Summon all the dust to rise,
Till it stir, and rub the eyes;
While this member jogs the other,
Each one whisp'ring, *Live you, brother?*

Come away,
Make this the day.
Dust, alas, no music feels,
But thy trumpet: then it kneels,
As peculiar notes and strains
Cure tarantula's raging pains.

Come away,
O make no stay!
Let the graves make their confession,
Lest at length they plead possession:
Flesh's stubbornness may have
Read that lesson to the grave.

Come away,
Thy flock doth stray.
Some to winds their body lend,
And in them may drown a friend:
Some in noisome vapours grow
To a plague and public woe.

Come away,
Help our decay.
Man is out of order hurl'd,
Parcell'd out to all the world.
Lord, thy broken consort raise,
And the music shall be praise.

# Judgement

Almighty Judge, how shall poor wretches brook
                 Thy dreadful look,
Able a heart of iron to appal,
                 When thou shalt call
For ev'ry man's peculiar book?

What others mean to do, I know not well;
                 Yet I hear tell,
That some will turn thee to some leaves therein
                 So void of sin,
That they in merit shall excel.

But I resolve, when thou shalt call for mine,
                 That to decline,
And thrust a Testament into thy hand:
                 Let that be scann'd.
There thou shalt find my faults are thine.

# Heaven

O who will show me those delights on high?
              *Echo.*        *I.*
Thou Echo, thou art mortal, all men know.
              *Echo.*        *No.*
Wert thou not born among the trees and leaves?
              *Echo.*        *Leaves.*
And are there any leaves, that still abide?
              *Echo.*        *Bide.*
What leaves are they? impart the matter wholly.
              *Echo.*        *Holy.*
Are holy leaves the Echo then of bliss?
              *Echo.*        *Yes.*

Then tell me, what is that supreme delight?
               *Echo.*       *Light.*
Light to the mind: what shall the will enjoy?
               *Echo.*       *Joy.*
But are there cares and business with the pleasure?
               *Echo.*       *Leisure.*
Light, joy, and leisure; but shall they persever?
               *Echo.*       *Ever.*


# Love (III)


Love bade me welcome: yet my soul drew back,
        Guilty of dust and sin.
But quick-ey'd Love, observing me grow slack
        From my first entrance in,
Drew nearer to me, sweetly questioning,
        If I lack'd anything.

A guest, I answer'd, worthy to be here:
        Love said, You shall be he.
I the unkind, ungrateful? Ah my dear,
        I cannot look on thee.
Love took my hand, and smiling did reply,
        Who made the eyes but I?

Truth Lord, but I have marr'd them: let my shame
        Go where it doth deserve.
And know you not, says Love, who bore the blame?
        My dear, then I will serve.
You must sit down, says Love, and taste my meat:
        So I did sit and eat.

# Notes

These notes are intended to explain archaic expressions and words which have since changed meaning, to help with difficult passages (like other poets, Herbert often condenses his thought), and to indicate Biblical texts which Herbert may well have had in mind and which can throw light on the verse. The dangers inherent in explanation – both of simplification and of complication – are barely avoidable, and the notes remain speculative and should not 'define' or restrict the reader's understanding and response. Herbert's poem are *poems*, original and inventive, always personal, not simply conventional glosses on Christian beliefs and practices. Commonly they relate to and evoke human experience in any place and in any age, no matter how secular the age or the reader.

**'The Thanksgiving':** **preventest:** anticipates, surpasses. **wept such store:** cf. Christ in the Garden of Gethsemane, Luke 22:44: 'being in an agony he prayed more earnestly: and his sweat was as it were great drops of blood falling down to the ground'. **door:** cf. John 10:9: 'I am the door: by me if any man enter in, he shall be saved.' **boxed:** struck; cf. John 19:3 'and they smote him with their hands', and the lines from Herbert's 'The Sacrifice': 'They buffet him, and box him as they list, / Who grasps the earth and heaven with his fist.' **My God, my God . . .:** cf. Matthew 27:46: 'My God, my God, why hast thou forsaken me?', Christ's last words on the cross. **posy:** bunch of flowers; also lines of poetry or motto. **passion:** the sufferings of Christ during his last days. **spital:** hospital, charitable home for the needy sick. **wit:** intelligence. **'tis here:** in this book of poetry. **thy book:** the Bible. **Thy art of love:** Christ's, i.e. not Ovid's *Ars Amatoria*.

**'The Reprisal':** **Reprisal:** retaliation, and also reprise, i.e. resumption of a theme in music, in this case the theme of the previous poem. **passion:** see above. **disentangled:** free of debt. **by thy death . . .:** being redeemed by your death, I am able to die for you.

**'The Agony':** **with a staff:** measured the distance as if with a surveyor's instrument. **repair:** go. **Mount Olivet:** Mount of Olives, specifically the Garden of Gethsemane, the scene of Christ's agony: see note to *wept such* *store* in 'The Thanksgiving'. **pike:** spear. **set . . . abroach:** pierce and leave running.

**'Redemption': new . . . lease:** cf. 'God, sending his own Son, hath wrought for us our Redemption: making us free from the law of sin and death, and granting us a *new small-rented lease.* This was purchased for us by, and granted to us at, the death of Christ' (George Ryley, 'Mr Herbert's Temple Explained', ms., 1715). Thus Christ's covenant as distinct from 'th' old' covenant between God and Moses.

**'Easter': calcined:** burnt to ashes, but also refined of impurities. **Consort:** play together on several instruments (here, 'heart and lute'). **twist:** weave, as in polyphonic music. **vi'd:** vied, increased in number by addition or repetition; the heart, the lute, and the 'blessed Spirit' make up the 'three parts' of a common chord. **I got me flowers . . .:** the song (though not 'long') promised above. **sweets:** as often in Herbert, perfumes.

**'Easter-wings': store:** abundance (of good things). **the fall:** the Fall of man, which occasioned the redemption by Christ. **imp:** strengthen a damaged wing by engrafting feathers (falconry).

**'Sin (I)': sorted:** assorted. **ties:** bonds.

**'Affliction (I)': tice:** entice. **Such stars:** cf. Luke 12:33: 'provide yourselves . . . a treasure in the heavens that faileth not, where no thief approacheth, neither moth corrupteth'. **made a party:** joined together (to create 'woe'). **My flesh began:** i.e. to complain. **edge:** appetite, desire for pleasure (cf. 'blunted knife'). **simp'ring:** perhaps in the modern sense of smiling foolishly or hypocritically; but 'simper' was an early form of 'simmer', to be on the verge of breaking out, in a state of suppressed agitation, suggesting half-heartedness. **academic:** briefly palliative; also suited to one 'wrapped in a gown'. **cross-bias:** causing to change direction (from bowls). **just:** serving a purpose.

**'Repentance': wormwood:** cf. Jeremiah 9:15: 'thus saith the Lord of Hosts . . . Behold, I will feed them, even this people, with wormwood.' **stay:** stay away. **bones:** cf. Psalm 51:8: 'Make me to hear joy and gladness; that the bones which thou hast broken may rejoice' (and 'Fractures well cur'd' below). Also, bones struck or rattled together as percussion instruments in music.

**'Prayer (I)':  in paraphrase:** 'In prayer the soul opens out and more fully discovers itself' (F. E. Hutchinson, *The Works of George Herbert*, 1941). **Engine against th' Almighty:** e.g. a battering-ram; see 'Artillery' below, 'we are shooters both', and notes. **transposing:** changing to a different musical key. **manna:** cf. Exodus 16:14–15: 'upon the face of the wilderness there lay a small round thing . . . And when the children of Israel saw it, they said one to another, It is manna: for they wist not what it was. And Moses said unto them, This is the bread which the Lord hath given you to eat.' **in ordinary:** as it always is, not needing to 'dress up' like man; or: 'ordinary', regular daily meal. **bird of Paradise:** believed to live entirely in the air, never touching the earth.

**'Antiphon':  Antiphon:** the chorus is sung by the congregation, the versicle by the minister.

**'Love (I)':  frame:** the universe. **parcell'd out:** divided into small portions. **scarf or glove:** articles of clothing that seduce ('warm') the eye; cf. an early sonnet of Herbert's: 'Doth poetry / Wear Venus' livery? only serve her turn? / Why are not sonnets made of thee? and lays / Upon thine altar burnt?'

**'Love (II)':  make thee way:** make way for thee. **pant:** pant after. **disseized:** dispossessed (legal).

**'The Temper':  Temper:** disposition ('the Christian temper'); also alluding to the hardening of steel and the tuning of a musical instrument. **spell:** contemplate, scan.

**'Jordan (I)':  Jordan:** the river in which Christ was baptized; symbolically, Herbert's dedication to a 'simple', truthful poetry. **veil'd:** partly hidden, as in pastoral allegory. (Herbert was far from averse to religious allegory.) **Shepherds:** writers of pastoral poetry; i.e. he has no great grudge against them. **pull for prime:** draw a winning hand in primero, a card game.

**'Employment (I)':  great doom:** Judgement Day. **great chain:** the 'Great Chain of Being', the hierarchy of Creation. **consort:** a company of musicians playing together.

**'The Holy Scriptures I':  thankful:** deserving gratitude. **ledger:** ambassador. **handsel:** foretaste, pledge.

**'The Holy Scriptures II':  make a motion:** refer the reader. **dispersed herbs do watch a potion:** possibly, herbs growing apart (pun on 'leaves' of the Scriptures) make a potion when combined; 'watch' may suggest watching for an opportunity. **Stars are poor books:** i.e. unreliable as interpreted by astrologers.

**'Whitsunday':  fire:** Pentecostal 'tongues of fire', the descent of the Holy Spirit ('sweet Dove') on the apostles. **twelve chosen men:** the apostles, the 'twelve suns' and 'pipes of gold' below. **braves:** threats, challenges.

**'Grace':  stock:** crops or cattle. **suppling:** softening.

**'Praise':  with a sling:** as used by David against Goliath. **next door . . . exalt the poor:** having reached the head, the effects of the potion 'dwell next door' to the soul, residing there. Exalted by God, the poor do better, they dwell near him: cf. 'Man is God's image; but a poor man is / Christ's stamp to boot' ('The Church-porch').

**'Sin (II)':  wants:** lacks. **being:** in theology, sin is non-being, absence, privation. **in perspective:** pictured, seen askew.

**'Church-music':  God help poor Kings:** because they are less happy than the music and the narrator. Rosemond Tuve (*A Reading of George Herbert*, 1952) cites Psalm 149:8, in which the saints are 'to bind their kings with chains'. **post:** depart.

**'The Church-floor':  neat and curious:** simple yet delicately wrought. **Could build so strong:** cf. I Corinthians 3:16: 'Know ye not that ye are the temple of God, and that the Spirit of God dwelleth in you?'

**'The Windows':  crazy:** flawed, disordered. **anneal:** to burn colours (into glass).

**'The Quiddity':  Quiddity:** the essence of a thing, that which makes it what it is. **Most take all:** 'A worldly proverb ("most" used in the sense of "the most powerful"), here christianized' (C. A. Patrides, *The English Poems of George Herbert*, 1974).

**'Avarice':  fain:** obliged. **the face of man:** the monarch's head stamped on coins.

**'Anagram'**: **Army ... pitch his tent:** cf. John 1:14: 'And the Word was made flesh, and dwelt among us'; Rosemond Tuve invokes The Song of Solomon 6:4: 'Thou art beautiful, O my love ... terrible as an army with banners.'

**'To All Angels and Saints'**: **after all your bands:** according to your various ranks. **in his hands:** cf. Isaiah 62:3: 'Thou shalt also be a crown of glory in the hand of the Lord.' **restorative:** gold was supposed to have medicinal powers. **cabinet:** cf. 'Anagram' above: 'did pitch his tent'. **I dare not:** a gently expressed opposition to Roman Catholic 'Mariolatry'. Helen C. White (*The Metaphysical Poets*, 1936) comments that the poem 'shows Herbert's feeling and imagination for once pressing against the bounds of his belief'. **prerogative:** i.e. the prerogative of God.

**'Employment (II)'**: **Quitting ... to:** leaving to. **complexions:** constitutions. **th' elements:** earth (the lowest, 'oppresst'), water, air and ('the highest') fire. **busy plant:** it blossoms and bears fruit simultaneously. **The man:** manhood, maturity.

**'Christmas'**: **With full cry:** in full cry, in pursuit. **expecting:** waiting. **rack:** a form of manger.

**'Sighs and Groans'**: **silly:** weak, pitiful. **Suck'd all thy magazines:** sucked dry all your storehouses; cf. what Herbert says, but approvingly, in *A Priest to the Temple:* the parson's chief knowledge derives from 'the book of books, the storehouse and magazine of life and comfort, the Holy Scriptures. There he sucks, and lives.' **Egyptian night:** the penultimate plague of God: 'and there was a thick darkness in all the land of Egypt three days' (Exodus 10:22). **fig-leaves:** as used by Adam and Eve to cover their nakedness after eating the forbidden fruit (Genesis 3:7). **vial:** cf. Revelation 15:7: 'seven vials full of the wrath of God'. **Cordial and corrosive:** respectively a comforting medicine and a caustic remedy.

**'Vanity'**: **spheres:** according to the Ptolemaic system of astronomy, the planets moved around the earth in nine concentric spheres. **full-ey'd aspects:** 'full' as in 'full moon', totally visible; cf. the final stanza of 'The Glance': 'Thy full-ey'd love'. **secret glances:** when visible only briefly or in part. **also hers:** the life of the prideful lady who would wear the pearl. **Chymick:** chemist, alchemist. **callow:** without feathers, i.e. not 'drest'.

**Embosoms in us:** cf. Jeremiah 31:33: 'I will put my law in their inward parts, and write it in their hearts.'

**'Virtue':** **sweets:** sweet things ('days and roses'), also perfumes. **coal:** cinders.

**'The Pearl':** **Matthew 13:** verses 45–6, 'the kingdom of heaven is like unto a merchant man, seeking goodly pearls: who, when he had found one pearl of great price, went and sold all that he had, and bought it.' **press:** as a wine or olive press, extracting the juice; here perhaps associated with the printing press. **conspire:** combine in their movements (perhaps, to exert their supposed influence on earthly affairs). **what forc'd by fire:** what nature reveals during scientific experiments, in contrast to 'willingly'. **Honour:** worldly esteem, social or professional standing. **vies of favours:** contests in doing favours (where one party or another prevails). **true-love-knot ... bear the bundle:** win the world, bind it, and carry it away. **spirit:** alcohol. **strains ... lullings ... relishes:** musical terms; as also **propositions:** *proposta*, theme of a fugue. **commodities:** profits, advantages accruing. **twist:** thread or cord to lead one out of a labyrinth.

**'Affliction (II)':** **a wonder:** cf. Psalm 71:7: 'I am as a wonder unto many; but thou art my strong refuge.'

**'Unkindness':** **coy:** reserved, retiring. **curious:** elegant. **pretendeth:** aspires (to a political appointment).

**'Submission':** **design:** intended goal of his life. **place and power:** cf. *A Priest to the Temple*: 'Ambition, or untimely desire of promotion to an higher state or place ... is a common temptation to men of any eminency.' **Disseize:** dispossess.

**'Justice (I)':** **skill of:** understand. **the hand:** the upper hand.

**'Charms and Knots':** **Knots:** knotty sayings. **Take one from ten ... :** a reference to the tithe (one-tenth of produce or income) paid annually by parishioners to the clergy, and its repayment (Herbert suggests) in the form of sermons.

**'Mortification':** **sweets:** perfumes. **clouts:** (swaddling) clothes. **attends:** awaits. **chair:** a sedan chair, carried between horizontal poles by two porters. **dress'd his hearse:** prepared his bier.

**'Jordan (II)':** **Jordan:** see note on 'Jordan (I)'. **lines:** of poetry. **quaint:** elaborate, ingenious. **burnish:** lengthen, spread out. **sped:** successful, satisfied. **quick:** alive, lively. **the sun:** also the Son. **friend:** cf. Christ in John 15:14–15: 'Ye are my friends . . . Henceforth I call you not servants . . . but I have called you friends.' **wide:** wide of the mark.

**'Prayer (II)':** **state:** high rank. **curse:** death; cf. Galatians 3:13: 'Christ hath redeemed us from the curse of the law, being made a curse for us.' **that which ti'd thy purse:** his divinity and hence immunity to death. **ell:** unit of length, about 45 inches.

**'Sion':** **Sion:** or Zion, the hill on which David built his city; i.e. Jerusalem. **Solomon's temple:** 'the house which king Solomon built for the Lord', described in I Kings 5–7. **within:** cf. Acts 7:47–8: 'Solomon built him an house. Howbeit the most High dwelleth not in temples made with hands', and I Corinthians 3:16: 'Know ye not that ye are the temple of God, and that the Spirit of God dwelleth in you?'

**'The Quip':** **Quip:** sharp sarcastic remark, or quibble. **train-bands:** trained (or largely untrained) companies of citizen soldiery. **But thou shalt answer . . .:** from Psalm 38:15 in the Book of Common Prayer.

**'The Dawning':** **Dawning:** of Easter Day (when Christ's followers came to the tomb). **burial-linen:** cf. Luke 24:12: 'Then arose Peter, and ran unto the sepulchre; and stooping down, he beheld the linen clothes laid by themselves.' **handkerchief:** also as miraculous means of healing, related of Paul in Acts 19:11–12; and cf. Revelation 21:4: 'God shall wipe away all tears from their eyes.'

**'Business':** **Business:** busyness. **two deaths:** the death of the body and that of the soul in hell; cf. Revelation 21:8: at the Last Judgement evildoers 'shall have their part in the lake which burneth with fire and brimstone: which is the second death'. **fee:** reward. **Two lives:** here and hereafter, both 'liv'd in misery'. **cross:** misfortune.

**'Dialogue':** **poise:** weight used in a pair of scales ('the balance'). **savour:** knowledge, understanding.

**'Dullness':** **curious:** elaborate. **quaint:** ingenious. **red and white:** red for blood, white for innocence, spotlessness. **window-songs:** serenades. **pretending:** wooing. **clear:** carry out the promise of, discharge.

*'Love-joy'*:  **Anneal'd:** burnt into, enamelled. **JESUS CHRIST:** cf. Christ, 'I am the true vine, and my Father is the husbandman . . . ye are the branches: he that abideth in me, and I in him, the same bringeth forth much fruit' (John 15:1–5).

*'Hope'*:  **watch:** indicating 'the brevity of human life, and the length of time already spent in waiting' (William Empson, *Seven Types of Ambiguity*, 1930). **anchor:** cf. Hebrews 6:19: 'Which hope we have as an anchor of the soul, both sure and steadfast.' **prayer-book:** 'prayer and an ordered way of life' (Empson). **optic:** telescope; 'The *optic* shows that their [the prayers'] fulfilment can only be descried afar off' (Hutchinson). **green ears:** 'which will need time to ripen for harvest' (Hutchinson). **ring:** of Christ the Bridegroom.

*'Time'*:  **wants:** lacks.

*'Gratefulness'*:  **occasion more:** an occasion for asking for more. **take:** win acceptance of, captivate. **spare days:** as it were, days off work, or niggardly, ungenerous days.

*'Peace'*:  **Prince of old:** Melchizedek, 'king of Salem . . . made like unto the Son of God; abideth a priest continually' (Hebrews 7:1–3); a prototype of, and here identified with, Christ. **Salem:** Jerusalem (Salem: Peace). **twelve stalks:** the apostles. **prosper'd . . . Through all the earth:** cf. Christ to the apostles: 'ye shall be witnesses unto me . . . unto the uttermost part of the earth' (Acts 1:8). **rehearse:** declare.

*'Confession'*:  **till:** drawer or smaller box. **rheums:** watery discharges. **foot:** grasp with the talons (of a hawk). **open breast:** confession. **cloudy to:** cloudy compared to.

*'Giddiness'*:  **snudge:** two senses: to be snugly quiet ('eat his bread in peace'), and to be miserly, sparing ('all day spares'). **scorns increase:** disdains to save, spends freely. **dolphin's skin:** iridescent when emerging from the water into the air; i.e. 'altering'.

*'The Bunch of Grapes'*:   **Grapes:** Moses' spies brought back grapes from Canaan as evidence of the land's fertility; cf. Numbers 13:24: 'The place was called the brook Eshcol, because of the cluster of grapes which the children of Israel cut down from thence.' **vogue:** general tendency. **Canaan . . . Red Sea:** 'The narrator enacts in his life the wanderings of the Israelites from *the Red Sea* to the Promised Land (*Canaan*)' (Patrides). **sea of shame:** possibly referring to the sea as symbolic of the Israelites' captivity in Egypt, or to their distrustful fears and rebellious 'murmurings' when camped before it (Exodus 14:10–12). **spann'd:** measured out. **sets us down:** prefigures our story. **let in:** anticipate, foretoken. **guardian fires and clouds:** cf. Exodus 13:20–21: 'they encamped . . . in the edge of the wilderness. And the Lord went before them by day in a pillar of a cloud, to lead them the way; and by night in a pillar of fire, to give them light.' **Scripture-dew:** manna; see note to 'Prayer (I)'. **shrouds:** temporary shelters. **murmurings:** complainings; cf. Exodus 16:2: 'the children of Israel murmured against Moses and Aaron in the wilderness.' **want:** lack. **I have their fruit:** see note to *'JESUS CHRIST'* in 'Love-joy': 'I am the true vine.' **Noah's vine:** cf. Genesis 9:20: 'Noah began to be an husbandman, and he planted a vineyard'; hence a prefiguration of Christ. **sweet wine:** the wine of the Communion and what it symbolizes.

*'Man's Medley'*:   **Medley:** a cloth woven with material of different colours; also a musical composition consisting of diversified parts. **pretence:** claim. **ties:** man alone combines the two lives, touching both earth and heaven. **round:** thick. **take place/After:** assume his rank according to. **ground:** coarse cloth basis (for the lace). **two winters:** the physical ('frosts') and the spiritual ('thoughts'). **two deaths:** see note to 'Business'.

*'The Storm'*:   **object:** lay bare, accuse them of. **Stars have their storms:** meteor showers.

*'Artillery'*:   **Artillery:** cf. Ephesians 6:13ff: 'take unto you the whole armour of God . . .', and 2 Corinthians 10:4: 'the weapons of our warfare are not carnal, but mighty through God'. **motions:** impulses. **shooters:** shooting stars. **shooters both:** warriors, archers. **articling:** bargaining, stipulating.

*'Justice (II)'*:   **of old:** before the redemption by Christ. **beam and scape:** respectively the crosspiece of the balance and the upright shaft. **Christ's pure veil:** Christ's flesh, as Hebrews 10:20: 'a new and living way, which

he hath consecrated for us, through the veil, that is to say, his flesh'; i.e. the New Covenant, between Christ and mankind.

*'The Pilgrimage'*: **strow'd:** strewed. **quicken'd by my hour:** spurred on by awareness of life's brevity. **wold:** uncultivated land. **angel:** gold coin; also guardian angel. **chair:** sedan chair, thus a comfortable way of travelling.

*'The Holdfast'*: **Holdfast:** cf. Hebrews 10:23: 'Let us hold fast the profession of our faith without wavering; for he is faithful that promised'; literally, a clamp, bolt, or other support holding a structure together. **What Adam had:** i.e. 'all things'.

*'The Discharge'*: **Discharge:** release from an obligation. **lickerous:** eagerly relishing. **counts:** accounts. **provide:** is provident of the future, 'spends thoughts and sense' on it. **breaks the square:** violates the proper order. **draw the bottom out an end:** as if unravelling a skein of thread to the end.

*'An Offering'*: **returns:** responses, reciprocations. **two natures:** divine and human. **one may be a nation, / And fence a plague:** one man may represent a nation and divert a pestilence upon himself: as David did (I Chronicles 21:17: 'Let thine hand, I pray thee, O Lord my God, be on me . . . but not on thy people, that they should be plagued').

*'The Bag'*: **Bag:** as it were, diplomatic bag. **close his eyes:** as Christ did on the boat during the tempest on the Sea of Galilee; Matthew 8:24: '. . . the ship was covered with the waves: but he was asleep'. **light:** alight. **tire:** head-dress. **fire:** lightning. **spear:** cf. John 19:34: 'one of the soldiers with a spear pierced his side.' **door:** see note to 'The Thanksgiving'.

*'The Collar'*: **Collar:** 'The title refers not to the modern clerical collar but to the common figurative expression, "to slip the collar" ' (Patrides); i.e. to escape, free oneself. Also a pun on 'choler', a fit of anger. **store:** abundance. **still in suit:** forever asking favours. **rope of sands:** i.e. unreal bonds. **wink:** close the eyes.

*'The Call'*: **Way . . . Truth . . . Life:** cf. John 14:6: 'Jesus saith unto him, I am the way, the truth, and the life.' **mends in length:** improves as it goes on. **move:** remove, take away.

**'Joseph's Coat'**: **Coat:** the 'coat of many colours' which Jacob made for Joseph (Genesis 37:3); hence symbolizing a father's love. **due to grief:** both body and heart being subject to grief. **ticing:** enhancing, making attractive.

**'The Pulley'**: **glass of blessings:** the poem inverts the Greek myth of Pandora ('all gifts') and her box, from which all the ills afflicting man were released, leaving behind hope as the only comfort. **span:** hand's-breadth.

**'Grief'**: **less world:** man, the microcosm. **feet:** a pun on metrical feet and the eyes 'running' with tears.

**'The Flower'**: **returns:** returnings, as the flowers in spring; also, that which is given. **demean:** demeanour; perhaps also demesne, possessions. **making a chiming:** making harmony; Hutchinson notes that a *passing-bell*, rung when someone was dying, was a single bell and hence did not *chime*. **Off'ring at:** aiming at. **to that:** can be compared to that. **glide:** slip away, perish.

**'Dotage'**: **glozing:** specious, misleading. **night-fires:** will-o'-the-wisps. **Chases in arras:** hunting scenes depicted in tapestry. **in a career:** unfolding swiftly. **in grain:** ingrained, rooted.

**'The Son'**: **coast:** i.e. whole region. **Chasing:** dispelling; i.e. a son perpetuates his father. **first man:** Adam.

**'A True Hymn'**: **behind:** lacking. **in kind:** in its true and proper nature.

**'A Dialogue-Anthem'**: **ancient sting:** cf. I Corinthians 15:55: 'O death, where is thy sting?' **void of story:** ignorant of history. **on him:** on Christ.

**'The Water-course'**: **sov'reign:** highly effective (as cure).

**'The Glance'**: **embalm:** anoint. **got the day:** won, prevailed.

**'Mary Magdalene'**: **Mary Magdalene:** cf. Luke 7:37–8: 'a woman in the city, which was a sinner . . . brought an alabaster box of ointment, and stood at his feet behind him weeping, and began to wash his feet with tears . . . and anointed them with the ointment.' **dash:** splash.

**'Aaron'**: **Aaron:** first high priest of the Israelites, thus typifying Christ's priestly role. (And relating to Herbert's.) **the old man . . . new drest:** cf. Colossians 3:9–10: 'seeing that ye have put off the old man with his deeds; and have put on the new man . . . after the image of him that created him.'

**'The Odour':** **2 Corinthians 2:** verse 15: 'For we are unto God a sweet savour of Christ.' **pomander:** mixture of aromatic substances made into a ball as a safeguard against infection; it releases its scent when warmed or squeezed ('worked', 'bruised'). **traffic:** work together (to their mutual enhancement).

**'The Forerunners':** **harbingers:** forerunners, advance party sent to secure lodgings for a royal progress, an army etc., who would mark the doors with chalk. Here the harbingers of old age and death 'chalk' the narrator's hair white. **dispark:** expel; also make dull (drive away the 'sparkle'). **pass not:** do not care. (As also in last stanza.) **stews:** brothels. **fond:** infatuated, foolish. **tic'd:** enticed, seduced. **canvas:** i.e. coarse cloth. **arras:** rich tapestry. **chalk:** see first note to the poem.

**'The Rose':** **Rose:** cf. 'the rose of Sharon' (The Song of Solomon 2:1), i.e. the Church. **size:** status, condition. **Colour'd:** disguised, made to seem what they are not. **purgeth:** roses were considered to have medicinal properties. **forbearance:** abstinence. **physic:** medicine.

**'Discipline':** **thy book:** the Bible. **man of war:** cf. Exodus 15:3: 'The Lord is a man of war.'

**'The Invitation':** **whose taste/Is your waste:** Hutchinson cites Isaiah 55:1–2: '. . . Wherefore do ye spend money for that which is not bread?' **feast:** the Eucharist, the sacrament commemorating the Last Supper, in which bread and wine (the body of Christ) are consecrated and consumed. **define:** characterize, limit. **cheer:** the feast; also gladness. **without:** outside.

**'The Banquet':** **Banquet:** the Eucharistic feast, as in the previous poem. **cheer:** as above. **neatness:** beauty, dignity, free from unnecessary embellishments. **Made a head:** advanced, to resist, subdue. **pomanders:** see note to 'The Odour'.

**'The Posy':** **Posy:** here, a motto, as inscribed on a ring. Cf. preface to *The Temple* by Nicholas Ferrar, of the religious community at Little Gidding, to whom Herbert had entrusted the manuscript: '. . . his own motto, with which he used to conclude all things that might seem to tend any way to his own honour: *Less than the least of God's mercies*'. And cf. Jacob's words in Genesis 32:10: 'I am not worthy of the least of all the mercies . . . which thou hast shewed unto thy servant.'

**'The Elixir'**: **prepossest**: to engage God's approval in advance, or to place his claim first. **his perfection:** its perfection. **his tincture: his:** its; *tincture*: in alchemy, supposedly an immaterial element or spiritual principle whose qualities might be infused into material things. **stone:** the 'philosophers' stone', a substance thought by alchemists to change base metals into gold. **touch:** test, as with a touchstone. **told:** counted.

**'Death'**: **fledge:** feathered, furnished for flight. **Half:** the body. **down, or dust:** the former if we sleep, the latter if we die.

**'Doomsday'**: **tarantula's raging pains:** referring to the hysterical malady supposedly caused by the bite of the tarantula spider, and thought to be cured by music ('notes and strains') and dancing. **make their confession . . . plead possession:** admit, despite the obstinacy they may have learnt from humans, that they cannot retain possession of bodies after the Last Judgement and the resurrection of the dead. **to winds their body lend:** their dust is scattered by winds which may cause shipwreck and 'drown a friend'. **noisome vapours:** pestilent gases. **consort:** see note to 'Employment (I)'; here, 'broken', out of harmony.

**'Judgement'**: **peculiar book:** individual record of good and bad actions. **thine:** because Christ took those faults upon himself. Cf. 'Love (III)': 'And know you not, says Love, who bore the blame?'

**'Heaven'**: **persever:** persevere, persist; pronounced 'perséver'.

**'Love (III)'**: **Love bade me welcome:** cf. 'The Invitation' and 'The Banquet', and the notes to these poems. Also Luke 12:37: God 'shall gird himself, and make them [his servants] to sit down to meat, and will come forth and serve them.'

# Everyman's Poetry

Titles available in this series **all at £1.00**

**William Blake**
ed. Peter Butter
0 460 87800 X

**Robert Burns**
ed. Donald Low
0 460 87814 X

**Samuel Taylor Coleridge**
ed. John Beer
0 460 87826 3

**Thomas Gray**
ed. Robert Mack
0 460 87805 0

**Ivor Gurney**
ed. George Walter
0 460 87797 6

**George Herbert**
ed. D. J. Enright
0 460 87795 X

**Robert Herrick**
ed. Douglas Brooks-Davies
0 460 87799 2

**John Keats**
ed. Nicholas Roe
0 460 87808 5

**Henry Wadsworth
Longfellow**
ed. Anthony Thwaite
0 460 87821 2

**John Milton**
ed. Gordon Campbell
0 460 87813 1

**Edgar Allan Poe**
ed. Richard Gray
0 460 87804 2

**Poetry Please!**
Foreword by Charles
Causley
0 460 87824 7

**Alexander Pope**
ed. Douglas Brooks-Davies
0 460 87798 4

**Lord Rochester**
ed. Paddy Lyons
0 460 87819 0

**Christina Rossetti**
ed. Jan Marsh
0 460 87820 4

**William Shakespeare**
ed. Martin Dodsworth
0 460 87815 8

**Alfred, Lord Tennyson**
ed. Michael Baron
0 460 87802 6

**R. S. Thomas**
ed. Anthony Thwaite
0 460 87811 5

**Walt Whitman**
ed. Ellman Crasnow
0 460 87825 5

**Oscar Wilde**
ed. Robert Mighall
0 460 87803 4